Queen Victoria's
Stalker

About the Author

Jan Bondeson is a senior lecturer and consultant rheumatologist at Cardiff University. His many critically acclaimed books include *Animal Freaks, Freaks: The Pig-Faced Lady of Manchester Square & Other Medical Marvels, Cabinet of Medical Curiosities, The London Monster* and the best-selling *Buried Alive: The Terrifying History of Our Most Primal Fear*. He lives in Newport, South Wales.

PRAISE FOR JAN BONDESON

Amazing Dogs
'A thrilling read - alternately hilarious and harrowing...
Bondeson aims to explode canine myths, but his most
surprising findings tend to validate them'
FELIPE FERNÁNDEZ-ARMESTO, *THE*
'Charming... a great story' CESAR MILLAN
(THE DOG WHISPERER), CESARWORLD.COM
'A fascinating new book' *THE DAILY MAIL*

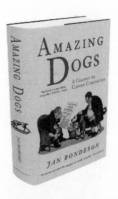

Greyfriars Bobby
'Greyfriars Bobby, the Victorian dog that held a 14-year
vigil at the grave of its master, is actually a myth... a
publicity stunt drummed up by local businessmen to
attract custom to their corner of Edinburgh'
THE DAILY TELEGRAPH

Buried Alive
'A little masterpiece of social history'
THE MAIL ON SUNDAY
'A wonderful book' *THE SUNDAY TELEGRAPH*

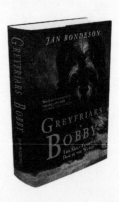

Animal Freaks
'Delightful' ALI SMITH
'Animal magic' *TLS*

Freaks
'Bizarre' *THE MAIL ON SUNDAY*
'Well written and superbly illustrated'
THE FINANCIAL TIMES

The London Monster
'Gripping... an 18th-century detective story of the most
piquant kind' *THE GUARDIAN*

Queen Victoria's Stalker

The Strange Story of the Boy Jones

JAN BONDESON

AMBERLEY

This edition first published 2012

Amberley Publishing
The Hill, Stroud
Gloucestershire, GL5 4EP

www.amberley-books.com

British Library Cataloguing in Publication Data.
A catalogue record for this book is available from the British Library.

ISBN 978-1-4456-0697-2

Typesetting and Origination by Amberley Publishing.
Printed in Great Britain.

Contents

Preface

'Un-easy is the head that wears
A Crown,' immortal Will declares;
And this is prov'd in our Queen's reign,
For 'the Tailor's Boy's got in again!'

How he gets in most puzzles all,
Through window is't? or over wall?
But down the Chimney *I* should state,
As that's the best way to the Great! (*grate*)
James Bruton, *The Boy wot enters the Palace.*

Most of us today think of Queen Victoria as an elderly, corpulent matron, dignified but quite forbidding-looking. But in 1838, she was young and not unattractive, just crowned Queen of her country, and still virginal and unmarried. Throughout Britain, there was widespread sympathy for, and curiosity about, the young Queen. Her coronation was viewed by huge and enthusiastic crowds, who were looking forward to her spring-like reign.

In contrast to these bright prospects, the newspapers of 1838 were full of murder, violence and mayhem. James Greenacre, who had murdered and dismembered his fiancée Hannah Brown, was convicted and hanged, but the equally gruesome murder of the young barmaid Eliza Davies, in Frederick-street, remained unsolved. The great murder news of 1838 concerned the beautiful prostitute Eliza Grimwood, who was found with her throat cut and her body viciously 'ripped' in late May. In spite of a multitude of clues linking various people with the murder, no person was ever convicted, and it remains a mystery to this day. In the 1838 newspapers, the various twists and turns of the Grimwood murder investigation competed for space with some sanguinary news from Kent, where the madman John Nichols Thom had staged some full-scale riots, and with the latest pranks of that fire-breathing, jumping horror, Spring-Heeled Jack.

Surely, the Queen herself would be safe from the murderers, madmen and fanatics infesting London and its environs? But her court at Buckingham Palace was run by well-nigh medieval standards by a number of inert functionaries, and no person was directly responsible for her security. Three groups of equally ineffective royal guardians operated independent of each other: the elderly and feeble royal porters, the royal pages who valued their night's sleep, and the military sentries who did not take their job very seriously.

This very slack regime was exposed by Queen Victoria's determined young stalker, the extraordinary 'Boy Jones', who developed an obsession with the young Queen. Time after time, he sneaked into Buckingham Palace to spy on her, sit on the throne, and rummage in her private apartments. 'Supposing he had come into the Bedroom, how frightened I should have been!' the fearful young Queen wrote in her Journal after the Boy Jones had been discovered lurking underneath a sofa in the room next to the one where she slept.

Several of Queen Victoria's biographers, including Lytton Strachey and Lady Longford, have briefly mentioned the Boy Jones.[1] Their opinions differ concerning how many times he broke into the palace, what his motives were, what measures were taken to rid the Queen of this persistent malefactor, and what happened to the Boy in the end. Some of them have concluded that there was only one Boy Jones, others that several Boys had a mania for entering Buckingham Palace at this time.[2] Although some other historians have attempted to find background material about Edward 'the Boy' Jones and his intrusions on royalty[3], this is the first true and complete account of that half-legendary character, one of the earliest celebrity stalkers in recorded history.

Queen Victoria's biographers have viewed the story of the Boy Jones and his multiple intrusions into Buckingham Palace as an amusing tale of a determined young boy who took on the establishment. The government, the Metropolitan Police, and the multitude of royal servants and pages at the palace were all equally powerless to stop the Boy Jones from stalking the young Queen. But it is in fact quite a dark and disturbing story, with the establishment striking back against the Boy with a vengeance, to make sure the Queen was safe from her persistent 'admirer'.

Charles Dickens, who once visited the Boy Jones in prison, knew his story well. It does not appear as if Dickens ever contemplated using it for the plot of one of his novels, perhaps because his enemy G. W. M. Reynolds beat him to it. This is a pity, since the Boy Jones himself comes across as a mix between Oliver Twist and Barnaby Rudge: a twisted innocent left to his own devices in a dangerous, hostile world full of perversion and intrigue. His elderly father rather resembles the grandfather of Little Nell, with regard to his lack of both intellect and judgement. There are villains aplenty, aiming for the downfall of our juvenile hero: a devious courtier, a choleric magistrate, an unconventional police inspector and a mean-spirited publican. But these dastardly players in the Boy Jones drama are only the chessmen of those far above them in rank: silent, grim-faced magnates who will stop at nothing in their quest to get rid of the Queen's bothersome stalker at any cost.

But these dangerous times in the life of the Boy Jones were but dark clouds on the horizon when he was one of the great criminal celebrities of London, giving interviews to the journalists from his prison cell. He would write a book about his observations at Buckingham Palace, he asserted, with a long chapter about what he had seen in the Queen's bedroom and dressing room. For reasons the reader will later appreciate, this bizarre autobiography was never written. But quoting what was alleged to be the Boy Jones's own words, I can exclaim, 170 years later:

> Yes, I will 'write a book' that will be read by great and small
> For seldom Truth before has scaled a Royal Palace wall;
> And never, I may safely say, has Prying gone so far
> As that of which I have to tell, in spite of prison bar;
> In spite of skilly diet, and the treadmill's grating jar.[4]

1

The Sweep in the Palace

When Lambert Jones kiss'd hands, so coy,
Says *Vic.*, but not with malice,
I wonder, *Al.*, if that's the *boy*
That got inside my palace?

From 'The Opening of the Royal Exchange' in J. Ashton (ed.), *Curiosities of Street Literature* (London, 1871)

At five o'clock in the morning of 14 December 1838, all seemed well at Buckingham Palace. One of the few people awake at this early hour was the night porter William Cox, on duty at the Equerry's Entrance. This entrance faced James-street, Pimlico, and the door was securely locked and bolted. Everything appeared to be very quiet this cold winter morning as the porter sat warming himself by the fireplace, hoping that none of the royal equerries would be rising early and that no visitor would be ringing the bell for his assistance.

Suddenly and unexpectedly, the door to the room opened and a face looked in at him. But what a face! It appeared to belong to a boy, but was black as coal and glistened like if it had been smeared with some greasy substance. The features were large and misshapen, the brow protruding, and the mouth extremely wide. As the stranger stood there in the doorway, silently grinning at him, William Cox must have been fearful that he was being haunted by Spring-Heeled Jack or some similar supernatural presence.

Having surveyed the startled porter for some time, the strange intruder calmly shut the door. The half-dazed William Cox sat pondering the situation for a little while, before bravely deciding to pursue the intruder. Whoever this strange being was, he certainly had no legitimate business in the Queen's palace. Cox lurched out into the corridor, shouting, 'Who are you? Have you come to sweep the flues?' but there was no answer and the mystery boy was nowhere to be seen. Instead, the porter almost stumbled over a large bundle, containing three pairs of trousers, a quantity of linen and undergarments, some foreign coins, a book and a padlock. There was also a fine dress sword marked with the name of the Hon. Charles Augustus Murray, one of Queen Victoria's equerries. Suspecting that the weird intruder had stolen this sword, Cox ran upstairs to Mr Murray's room and knocked on the door. Since there was no response, he opened the door with his master key, rightly suspecting that Mr Murray was away. The porter was shocked to find the room in a dreadful state: the furniture was liberally sprinkled with soot, and the bedlinen was very much besmirched with soot and grease, like if the intruder had been rolling around in the bed. On the dressing-table, a large, half-empty bottle of bear's grease showed obvious marks of soot, indicating that its contents had been 'used' by the mystery boy.[1]

Probably feeling somewhat relieved that he was really dealing with a thief rather than some ghost or devil, Cox woke up a number of his colleagues and alerted the sentries. After one of the porters had been dispatched to fetch some police constables, Cox and the others searched the corridors and staterooms for the intruder. They found traces of soot in several of the bedrooms and passages, and in the Marble Hall itself. A valuable likeness of the Queen was found on the floor of the Marble Hall, broken and covered with soot. Underneath it were two letters, one addressed to her Majesty personally, the other to the Hon. Mr Murray; marks of soot and grease indicated that the intruder had opened and read both of them. There must have been shivers down the spine of William Cox when he realised that the intruder had actually entered the Queen's private apartments and stolen the letter. It was fortunate that Queen Victoria had been staying at Windsor Castle that fateful night.

Two police constables, who had fortuitously been on patrol in James-street itself, now joined the search. One of them, a jolly-looking fellow named James Stone, 81B, found Cox's story most amusing. He suggested that Cox had been just been 'seeing things', or even that he might have enjoyed a toddy too many and nodded off on his watch, but the indignant porter showed him the stolen goods and the filthy room, saying that it was no joking matter that the Queen's palace was burgled and vandalised. As the search party was trudging downstairs after another futile search of the bedrooms and corridors, Constable Stone saw something move behind a pillar in the Marble Hall. Signing to the others that they should not make any alarm, he sneaked up to the pillar and collared the intruder. Just like the porter before him, Stone was amazed how grotesque the boy looked with his grinning blackened face and white staring eyes. Since his clothes were liberally smeared with grease, the intruder was able to wriggle free and take to his heels.

A ludicrous chase ensued, the porters and policemen stumbling around in the half-darkness and sometimes cannoning into each other. The boy made his way out through a window, and ran out onto the lawn, but Constable Stone pursued and recaptured him after a long chase and hauled him back into the palace. When the boy was dragged into the kitchen where the lighting was better, the kitchen-maids gave a collective yell when they saw this stunted, repulsive-looking creature being ushered along by the porters and police. William Cox declared that he was certainly the same boy who had stood grinning at him earlier in the morning. When his pockets were searched, they were found to contain a wafer, a stamp, and two inkstand glasses, both smeared with soot and grease. He wore two pairs of trousers, one on top of the other, and two overcoats. When the outer pair of trousers were pulled down by the police constable, several items of female underwear tumbled out, to the great indignation of everyone present.

The boy gave his name as Edward Cotton, adding that he came from Hertford, where his father was a respectable tradesman. When the police constables asked him why he had entered Buckingham Palace, how long he had been there, and by what means he had been able to sneak into the palace, the boy remained stubbornly silent. In the early morning hours, he was removed to the Queen-square police office, where the constables took evidence from the palace porters and tried to reconstruct the mystery boy's movements. Somehow, possibly through a chimney, they mused, the boy had made his way into the palace, strolling through the staterooms, corridors and bedrooms like if they had belonged to him. Showing remarkable knowledge of the layout of the palace, as well as a superior sense of direction, he had entered the Queen's empty bedroom and dressing room, where he had stolen her portrait, a letter addressed to her, and some items of linen and underwear. He had then searched some other empty bedrooms before entering that of the Hon. Mr Murray. Here, he had opened a large bottle of bear's grease and smeared himself with its contents, possibly in a futile attempt to aid his escape through the chimney. After rolling on the bed and sprinkling soot all over the room, he had stolen a variety of other objects from the rooms of Mr Murray and his German servant Frederick Blume, before going down to frighten William Cox by peering into his room early in the morning.

We must now briefly leave the mysterious 'Edward Cotton' to rattle the bars of his prison cell at the Queen-square police office, in order to provide a historical background to his weird activities. Queen Victoria's accession to the throne in 1837 had changed the people's perception of monarchy quite profoundly. Neither George IV nor William IV had been particularly popular monarchs, and there had been jubilations when the reactionary Duke of Cumberland succeeded to the throne of Hanover and left Britain for good. Many people felt that Victoria's accession heralded a new era in the history of England, free of the corruption, waste and excesses for which her wicked uncles had become notorious. There was a widespread feeling of sympathy for the Queen, since she was young, not unattractive, and politically innocent. The youthful Victoria basked in a revival of royal populism: there were many books, pamphlets and poems heralding the beginning of her spring-like reign.

Many of the publications glorifying the young Queen dwelt at length on her great wisdom, goodness and sense of philanthropy, and also her superior personal attractions.[2] Although her looks owed more to youth than to regularity of features or shapeliness of figure, the published prints and drawings of her all presented her as a beauty. A popular ballad of the times even claimed that

> Of all the flowers in full bloom
> Adorn'd with beauty and perfume
> The fairest is the rose in June
> Victoria Queen of England![3]

In January 1838, the *Spectator* derided the craze of Regina-mania, where even commentators who should have known better kept on flattering the Queen's every attraction, 'dwelling constantly on the beauty not only of the Queen's face and features, but of her feet and even of her slippers'.[4] But this warning came too late for the many young men who had already fallen in love with the young Queen. Those timid and fearful of ridicule sat in their parlours sighing over Victoria's portrait; the more robust admirers threw amorous epistles into her carriage as she drove by; the boldest and least sane of them even had the temerity to call at Buckingham Palace to demand her hand in marriage. Charles Dickens made a joke that he and two of his friends were in love with the Queen, like so many others. They wore marriage medals next to their hearts, had their pockets full of the Queen's portrait, which they wept over in secret, and drove to Windsor Castle to admire the royal bedchamber. Dickens had read a newspaper report about a certain John Stockledge, who had demanded to be admitted to Windsor Castle, since he was looking for a wife and thought the Queen would do very well.[5]

The early Victorian police was organised into divisions, each of which had a certain territory to patrol. It was the 'A' or Westminster division that had the duty of protecting the royal family. From a police memorandum entitled 'Return of All Persons who have come under cognizance of the Police Force for Offences against Her Majesty Queen Victoria', much can be learnt about the Queen's persistent admirers.[6] Count Dombriski, a Polish officer who had received a musket wound at Waterloo, threw a letter into the Queen's carriage in July 1837. He was watched by the police for some time before he went to America. In January 1838, a madman named Patrick Lynden tried to enter Buckingham Palace to deliver a letter to his beloved Queen Victoria; when he was apprehended by two police constables, he furiously assaulted them. Lynden was confined in Bedlam. Just a few weeks later, a middle-aged man named Arthur Tucker, 'whose appearance was that of a horse dealer', tried to enter Buckingham Palace through the tradesman's entrance. When challenged, he said he knew about a sinister conspiracy against the Queen and the Duchess of Kent. Tucker was discharged into the care of his brother, who promised to keep an eye on him.[7]

But not all the people with an abnormal interest in the young Queen had such benign intentions. When the Queen's carriage was proceeding through Birdcage Walk in November 1837, a respectably dressed gentleman with a star on his breast shook his fist and shouted 'You damned ___, you usurper, I'll have you off the throne before this day week!' among other highly insulting and seditious expressions. When arrested, he turned out to be Captain John Goode, 'a fine, handsome-looking man, of dark complexion, and in his forty-first year'. Coming from a wealthy and respectable Devon family, he had served in the 10th Foot for quite a few years, before developing the delusion that he was the son of George IV and Queen Caroline and thus King John II, the lawful sovereign of England. On trial, he declared that if he were allowed near the Queen, he would tear her to pieces. He also wanted to empty all the royal tombs and scatter the bones, and to hang and disembowel all traitors, particularly the members of the Russian and Danish embassies. When taken away in a coach after being sentenced to be confined in Bedlam, he smashed all the windows and yelled out 'Guards of England, do your duty and rescue your sovereign!' to the astonishment of the bystanders. Captain Goode was transferred to Broadmoor in 1864; he died there, a wreck of a man, in 1883, maintaining his delusion to the last.[8]

Captain Goode was not the only individual threatening Queen Victoria in late 1837. Charles Stuber, had once been a prosperous baker, the master of a large bakery in Chelsea as well as three other houses, but as a newspaper expressed it, 'a second marriage to a female much younger destroyed all his prospects'. The ruined baker, who had to work as a journeyman to more prosperous colleagues, spent much time ruminating over his financial collapse. Concluding that he was the victim of a vast conspiracy led by the Queen and her mother the Duchess of Kent, Stuber wrote some extremely violent and threatening letters to them. Since he had given his name and address, it was not difficult for the police to track him down. When arrested, the sinister German exclaimed, 'They've taken me just in time – they've saved a dreadful murder – I would have done it, for we don't want Kings and Queens in this country!' Like Captain Goode, Stuber was confined in an asylum.[9]

On 11 July 1838, the porters of Buckingham Palace were shocked to discover a man sleeping peacefully in a chair in the Picture Gallery, situated just seven yards from the Queen's bedroom. He turned out to be the silversmith Thomas Flower, one of the many people who had developed an obsession with the young Queen. He had twice been bound over to keep the peace for trying to approach Queen Victoria, once trying to obtain entrance to her box at the opera-house. Flower said he had come to ask the Queen's hand in marriage, but he had fallen asleep after having searched in vain for her bedroom. He must have missed her by a very narrow margin, since the Queen had passed through the corridor to her bedroom just ten minutes before Flower was apprehended. The silversmith had a reputation as a respectable man, with the caveat that 'when under the influence of liquor, he becomes a most dangerous lunatic'. Flower was sent to Tothill-fields Prison, but two of his friends bailed him out for £50, he himself providing another £50 and a promise to keep the peace. This did not stop Flower from further outrageous behaviour, however. In early September, Sergeant Nixon of the 'B' Division saw the drunken Flower walking in Jew's-row, Chelsea. His ambition to marry the Queen must have been of short duration, since he was in the company 'with two of the lowest description of prostitutes'. Thinking that Flower might be robbed, the sergeant watched him. All of a sudden, Flower's wife came running up 'and endeavoured to conciliate him', but the caddish husband aimed a kick at her. When Sergeant Nixon collared Flower, he was swiftly knocked down, kicked and jumped on by the infuriated silversmith. When he was tackled by another policeman, Flower bit him hard in the thigh. Rather understandably, none of the friends who had previously forfeited their bail came forward on Flower's behalf for a second time, and since he was now penniless himself, he was sent to prison.[10]

Exactly how Thomas Flower had managed to get inside Buckingham Palace was never ascertained, but the walls were low, with many overhanging tree branches. It was of regular occurrence that tramps and drunken soldiers were found sleeping in the palace gardens. As signified by the Flower and 'Edward Cotton' incidents, the security at Buckingham Palace was abysmal.[11] Although the year was 1838, the Royal Household was run by medieval standards, by a number of inert functionaries. The office of the Lord Chamberlain was responsible for maintaining parts of the palace, that of the Lord Steward for others. This division of duties led to the most farcical situations: for example, the office of the Lord Chamberlain provided lamps, that of the Lord Steward cleaned and trimmed them, and that of the Master of the Horse made sure they were lit. The insides of the royal windows were cleaned by the Lord Chamberlain's department, the outsides by the Office of Woods and Forests; the cleaning was never done simultaneously, meaning that the Queen had to gaze through windows that were translucent only.

The housekeepers, pages and housemaids at Buckingham Palace were under the authority of the Lord Chamberlain; footmen, livery porters and under-butlers were under the Master of the Horse; the 445 remaining palace servants were controlled by the Lord Steward. Once, when the Queen demanded a dining-room fire to be lit, she was gravely answered by an official representing the Lord Steward that this could not be done, since he was only responsible for laying the fire; lighting it was the department of the Lord Chamberlain. To make things even worse, the Lord Chamberlain, Lord Steward and Master of the Horse were sinecure appointments given to distinguished noblemen who no longer lived at court; they delegated authority to servants very inferior in rank. These individuals jealously guarded their ancient privileges and resented trespass into the customary preserves of their departments. The mean age of the royal servants was high. They had been chosen through a corrupt 'grace and favour' system and kept in their posts until well past retirement age. Many of the footmen and porters were timorous old men who appreciated their night's sleep. Others were lazy scoundrels who enjoyed their lack of supervision and drank, smoked and slept on duty.

No person was responsible for security at Buckingham Palace: the Lord Chamberlain had no authority over the porters, and the Lord Steward had nothing to do with the disposition of the pages. The army sentries had their own officers, who did not liaise with the court functionaries, and who often took their duties lightly. The Flower outrage prompted a reinforcement of the police presence at Buckingham Palace: two inspectors, a sergeant and six constables, all from the 'A' Division, were permanently stationed there, even in the absence of her Majesty. One must presume that at least some of these royal guardians were supposed to be on duty also during night-time, but embarrassingly enough, this does not seem to have been the case the night Edward Cotton was apprehended. The police constables who eventually arrived at the scene were from the 'B' division and had fortuitously strayed out of their own territory, to be called by the desperate royal porters early in the morning. The only involvement of the 'A' division was that, early in the morning, Police Constable W. Badcock, 58A, had been called to the tradesman's entrance to help escort the boy to the Queen-square police office.

The morning after his arrest, Edward Cotton remained as truculent as ever, objecting vociferously when the constables tried their best to clean him up. Since he still refused to divulge why he had entered Buckingham Palace, the policemen decided to take him before the magistrate, in the hope that this official would be able to loosen the mystery boy's tongue.[12] When facing the presiding magistrate, Mr White, 'Edward Cotton' looked marginally less repulsive, although his clothes were still very dirty. The newspaper reporters described him as a stunted, ugly-looking boy, whose appearance was that of a chimney sweep. In contrast to his secretive demeanour when questioned by the police, he willingly gave his name and what he claimed was the Hertford address of his father Henry Cotton, and answered Mr White's questions without hesitation. He explained that when he had come to London twelve months earlier, he had met a man in a fustian jacket who asked him to go to Buckingham Palace. This man had got him past the palace guards, letting him into the royal residence. The stern Mr White commented that it was a most extraordinary thing that persons could get into the palace under such circumstances. The Boy went on to say that, since he had come to London 'to better himself', he considered himself 'very well off'.

'Well, you could not go to a higher place!' Mr White interceded.

'I declare it to be the case, and I lived very well,' the Boy replied calmly.

During daylight hours, Edward had been hiding behind the furniture or up the chimneys, he said. When night came, he walked about at will. He had been living off 'victuals in the kitchen' and had washed his only shirt at regular intervals. He had always been present when the Queen had a meeting with the Ministers, hiding behind some furniture in the room, and heard just about everything they had to say ...

'Do you mean to tell me that you have lived in the Palace *upwards of eleven months*, and been concealed when Her Majesty held a Council?'

'I do.'

'Were you hid behind a chair?

'No. But the tables and other furniture concealed me.'

'Then you could hear all Her Majesty said?'

'Oh, yes. And her Ministers too.'

The Boy said that, in Hertford, he had lived with Henry Cotton, a shoemaker and householder.

'Is he any relation?' asked the stern Mr White.

'Only my father!' answered the facetious Boy, amidst renewed laughter from the audience.

'You are a sweep, are you?'

'Oh no, it is only my face and hands that are dirty; that's from sleeping in the chimneys. I do not know the names of any of the servants, but I know my way all over the palace, and have been all over it, the Queen's apartments and all.'

As 'the prisoner, who evidently seemed to think the whole proceeding good fun, was removed from the bar', the journalists present in court could scent a sensational story. Had this grubby urchin really been living in Buckingham Palace for nearly a year, spying on its every secret? And what had he seen in the Queen's private apartments? In spite of his revolting appearance, he had seemed quite intelligent, and entirely sane. They thought his answers had been given in a shrewd and reasonable manner, signifying that he possessed some education. There was much speculation how old the Boy was, with guesses ranging from fifteen up to twenty-four years.

After having been examined by the magistrate, Edward Cotton was taken to the Tothill-fields Bridewell prison, where he could be kept in safe custody while inquiries were made concerning his sensational claims. Inspector Steed, of the 'A' Division, disbelieved the Boy's story that he had been in the palace for nearly a year, however. It would hardly have been possible for him to obtain victuals from the kitchen over such a long period of time, particularly since the larders and cupboards were locked by the under-butlers when the servants retired to bed. The Boy had stated that he frequently washed his shirt at night, but that would hardly have been possible when all fires and lights were extinguished, and no water available. He could have been in the palace for at most two or three days, the Inspector concluded.[13]

Since the short and dirty Edward Cotton looked just like a chimney sweep's boy, the police suspected that he had been one of the climbing boys employed by the Buckingham Palace sweep and that he had become acquainted with the location and layout of the Queen's private apartments through climbing down their chimneys. He could then have returned at night, gained access to the roof, located the right chimney, and climbed down into the Queen's bedroom or dressing room, before setting out on his nightly ramble through Buckingham Palace. But Mr Williams, the Chimney Sweeper to Her Majesty, denied ever having seen, or employed, the Boy. This experienced chimney sweep also told the police that it was not possible for any human being to enter Buckingham Palace by climbing down the chimneys, since they had been deliberately constructed to prevent this from happening. It would have been possible for the Boy to have hidden inside the chimneys during daylight hours, however, but this would have been an extremely dangerous scheme in cold December weather. If someone had lit a roaring fire underneath him, he would have been scorched by the flames or suffocated by the smoke.

Inquiries were also underway regarding the Boy's origins and parentage. From his accent and general demeanour, he seemed like a London street lad of the lower classes, and certainly very unlike a country bumpkin from Hertfordshire. Since a workforce of more than 100 labourers was employed at Buckingham Palace, making some alterations during the Queen's absence, the police suspected the Boy might have sneaked in with them. Most of those workmen were taken to Tothill-fields to be confronted with the Boy, but none of them knew him. After it had been decided to advertise in the newspapers to find out if some Londoner was missing an adventurous teenage boy, the Boy received a torrent of visitors, many of whom came to see him as a curiosity.

Among the crowd of people coming to see the mystery boy was a grey-haired, shabbily dressed man, who introduced himself as Henry Jones, a tailor living in Bell-yard, York-street. His fourteen-year-old son Edward had gone missing a week earlier, he said. Edward had attended school until early in 1836, when he quit school to become errand-boy to an apothecary. When sacked from this position due to his 'mischievous and restless disposition', he instead became a builder's boy at Mr Griffiths' builder's office in Coventry-street, Haymarket. Here he did slightly better and lasted more than a year, before recently being sacked by his employer after enjoying one prank too many. Edward was of a lazy disposition and preferred to lounge about back home, old Jones explained. He showed no urgency to gain employment, and his perpetual bad conduct had led to an angry quarrel, during which Jones senior turned his errant son out of doors, saying that he was now old enough to fend for himself. Afterwards, Henry Jones had regretted this rash action, since Edward did not return home. After a week had gone by, old Jones became fearful that Edward had drowned himself, although this does not seem to have induced him to actively search for his son or even to report his disappearance to the police. But when the tailor saw the newspaper stories about the mysterious 'Edward Cotton' breaking into Buckingham Palace, he recalled that Edward had always been talking about the Queen and other royal personages and their grand life at the palace, and decided to go and see the mystery boy at the police office.

This sounded promising, the police constables thought, and Henry Jones was allowed to see the prisoner. The moment he set eyes on the boy, he declared that this was certainly his absconded son Edward. In spite of the lack of paternal affection he had shown earlier, the old tailor seemed genuinely pleased to see the boy, although the latter did not reciprocate, refusing to answer any questions and looking as truculent as ever. The police constables were a little suspicious, since Henry Jones looked at least sixty years old, and hardly fit to have such a young son. And could this grim-faced troglodyte of a boy really be just fourteen years old? They sent for the builder Mr Griffiths, the man named by Henry Jones as Edward's most recent employer, and this respectable tradesman immediately recognised the Boy as his former apprentice.

On 19 December, Edward Jones, otherwise Edward Cotton, was again placed at the bar at the Queen-square police office, before the magistrates Mr White and Mr Gregorie, charged with stealing a sword and various other articles, the property of the Hon. Charles Augustus Murray, Master of Her Majesty's Household. The fact that he had also stolen a private letter to Queen Victoria, her portrait, and a quantity of linen and female underclothes, was not even alluded to. Since the story of the Boy living concealed inside Buckingham Palace for nearly a year had become widely known and created much curiosity, the office was completely crowded. Many journalists were present, as were the Hon. Mr Byng and others of distinction. A journalist from *The Era* newspaper paid tribute to the acrid soap and bristly brushes used by the Queen-square constables when he commented that 'the boy's appearance when placed in the dock was very different from that on the former occasion. The whole of the soot and grease with which he had bedaubed himself had been washed off at the prison, and he exhibited an open and intelligent countenance.'[14]

The porter William Cox was the first witness, testifying about his alarming nocturnal encounter with the intruder. He had no idea how the Boy had been able to enter Buckingham Palace, nor how he could have acquired such accurate knowledge regarding its internal layout. He believed the Boy had hoped to escape through the Equerry's Entrance, but he had panicked when perceiving this door was securely locked with a porter in attendance, had dropped some of his loot and run out into the Marble Hall.

Inspector Steed was the second witness. After having surveyed the various entrances to Buckingham Palace, he rather suspected the Boy might have slid underneath the Marble Arch gateway, where there was sufficient space to admit a short boy without any particular inconvenience.

'And is there no sentry at this entrance?' inquired Mr White.

'There are two!' replied the policeman.

The inspector went on to explain that he had examined the Boy's boots and found some pieces of gravel that exactly corresponded with that laid down near the Marble Arch entrance.

The aforementioned builder Thomas Griffiths declared that he had gone to Tothill-fields, where he had recognised the prisoner as his former errand-boy Edward Jones, presumed to be sixteen years old (he was in fact only fourteen). Edward had always been of a particularly imaginative and fanciful turn of mind, the builder explained, and he had often spoken about wanting to see the grand staircase at Buckingham Palace. Mr Griffiths had never guessed that this menial lad would one day actually fulfil his ambition! Although Henry Jones, who was probably ashamed about turning his son out of doors, did not give evidence, the journalists had found out that the Boy was 'the son of a poor tailor of dissipated habits, who has a family of seven children, and resides in Bell-yard, York-street.'[15]

Finally, Mr White sternly asked Edward Jones whether he had anything to say. Looking as truculent as ever, the Boy calmly stated that since he had always wished to see the palace, he had sneaked up to the tradesman's entrance of the left wing, entering undetected behind a man with a fustian jacket. This was at five in the afternoon of Tuesday 11 December, and he had thus had several days to 'range over the palace without molestation', as he expressed it, before being caught early on Friday 14 December. Pointing at the stolen goods, Mr White asked, 'Why did you middle with these articles?'

Edward Jones began a rambling tale about finding all these articles on the lawn, but the magistrate had heard such yarns before and curtly snapped, 'I am going to send you for trial.'

'Oh, very well, with all my heart,' replied the Boy, with the greatest composure.

The second examination of Edward Jones at the police office cannot have been an uplifting experience for Henry Jones and the Boy's other friends. The evidence for the prosecution seemed rock solid, their witnesses spoke up against the palace intruder without hesitation, and poor Edward himself appeared evasive and untruthful. Even the timid, sluggish-witted Henry Jones realised that unless an experienced barrister was employed as the prisoner's friend, Edward's chances of escaping a lengthy prison sentence, or even transportation to Australia, were extremely slim. The problem was that old Jones was almost penniless. He rented a mean little tailor's shop in Derby-street, Parliament-square, but he either was not a very good tailor or else lacking in industry; his considerable fondness for drinking beer cannot have helped the situation at all. As a result, his family was living hand to mouth. Having married late in life, Henry Jones still had not less than seven children alive, of whom Edward, the eldest, was fourteen years old and the twins Julia and Mary just two.

The entire Jones family lived in a single room, situated in Bell-yard, York-street, Westminster. Behind a large and prosperous tavern known as the Bell was Bell-yard, a narrow passage with dark, unsanitary-looking buildings on each side, where the damp, dirty rooms were rented by the Joneses and other equally penurious people. Like a proper slum lord, the proprietor of the Bell, Mr William James, had been able to cram not less than fifty-one souls into this dismal rookery.[16] Since his family had lived in Bell-yard for several years, Henry Jones went to explain his plight to Mr James, but the Scrooge-like publican refused to lend him a penny. Old Jones should forget all about his criminal son, Mr James advised nastily, and concentrate on paying his rent punctiliously, something he had not always found easy in the past. But just like in a Charles Dickens novel, the other poor people in this part of Westminster did what they could to help Henry Jones and his son. Having read or heard about the Buckingham Palace intruder, they willingly lent what they could to support the underdog: Henry Jones borrowed a shilling here, a penny there, until he had five guineas, enough to afford the services of the eloquent Mr William Prendergast, Barrister-at-Law.

On 27 December 1838, the Westminster Quarter Sessions began at the Guildhall, before Mr Serjeant Adams, Chairman, and a full Bench of Magistrates.[17] After the grand jury had been sworn, Serjeant Adams addressed them. He expressed his regret that the calendar should present such a long list of malefactors. Among them, the most peculiar by far was the case of the chimney sweeper found in Buckingham Palace, which had attracted so much newspaper publicity. The jury should not be confounded by this 'very considerable public attention', however, since the law was the same for a cottage as for a palace, and the case of the Sweep in the Palace should be determined by 'an ordinary and straightforward inquiry'.

Mr Serjeant Adams again showed a praiseworthy zeal for democracy in allowing a number of very ordinary criminals precedence over the palace intruder; in fact, the trial of Edward Jones only began on 28 December.[18] Mr (later Sir) William Bodkin prosecuted on behalf of the Board of Green Cloth, an archaic congregation of senior court officials, named after the green baize table where they used to confer. The charge was that of having stolen, on 14 December, a sword belonging to the Hon. Charles Augustus Murray, and three pairs of trousers, and other articles, the property of Frederick Blume. When Mr Bodkin addressed the crowded Guildhall in ringing tones, things were not looking good for Edward Jones. Mr Bodkin would call witnesses who would testify that the Boy had entered Buckingham Palace unlawfully and taken various articles with the intent of converting them to his own use. He entreated the jury to disregard all the foolish stories spread about by the prisoner himself: this was a simple case of theft and should be treated and punished as such.

The first witness was the porter William Cox, who repeated the story about finding the boy and retrieving the sword and 'several articles of wearing apparel', as he cautiously expressed it. Clearly, the witnesses had been instructed to avoid mentioning the Queen's portrait, letter and underclothes at all costs. When Cox produced two inkstand glasses and a wafer stamp, which had been found on the prisoner when he was arrested, it was time for Mr Prendergast to interfere. Theatrically holding up the inkstand glasses, which were extremely dirty and discoloured, he exclaimed, 'Oh, no, he cannot mean that! These things belong to the Queen? Oh! I cannot believe it.'

There was loud laughter as Mr Bodkin tried to rescue the witness by reminding the jury that although these objects technically belonged to the Queen, she was not in the habit of using them.

'I should think not, indeed!' exclaimed the mock-indignant Mr Prendergast.

Cox went on to admit that when the prisoner was questioned, he airily said that he had always wanted to see the palace, and had come for that objective only. It also transpired that Mr Bodkin had yesterday been taken for a guided tour through the palace, to see for himself where the Boy had made his mischief. The waggish Mr Prendergast again provoked much laughter when he asked Cox whether anything had been missed from the palace since his learned friend's visit; the sheepish-looking porter, who did not understand the joke, could only confirm that this was not the case.

Two police constables next described how the Boy had been captured. Detailing the various goods that had been purloined, they mentioned the dirty pot of bear's grease, which looked like it had recently been 'used'. The Boy had said he had lived in the palace for twelve years, but when the policeman expressed incredulity, he had changed this to twelve months. The German valet Frederick Blume, whose English was not very good, tried his best to describe the state of the room and the various items purloined by the Boy. He repeatedly spoke of the 'marks of soot' in his guttural accent, and the jolly Mr Prendergast overheard this as 'Marshal Soult', expressing surprise that this celebrated French general and statesman had also made his way into Buckingham Palace!

There was more buffoonery when Mr Prendergast examined the various foreign coins found in Blume's japanned tin box. The policeman asserted that they were foreign *sous* pieces, but it turned out that Blume had been collecting some very odd coins. One had the image of the Duke of Wellington, with the inscription 'By trampling on Liberty I lost the Throne' and looked very much like a counterfeit coin. Another was a Dutch coin, bearing on it the likeness of William of Nassau.

When Blume was called to explain another bogus-looking coin, he exclaimed, in his foreign accent, 'Oh that? That was once a sovereign, but I afterwards put it into a fire, and it turned into a farthing!'

There was again much laughter at the unfortunate valet, who had been conned by a gilt farthing. The German became so confused he could not even swear that the coins were his, only that his box had contained some coins that rather resembled those examined. Some degree of order was restored when the clerk of the Queen-square police office read the protocol detailing the Boy's various lies, beginning with the story of his being born in the palace and spending twelve years there, and ending with his allegation that he had found the stolen goods on the lawn.

Then it was time for the jolly Mr Prendergast to perform. With a pointed reference to the omission of the various articles purloined from the Queen's bedroom, he declared himself very pleased that, contrary to what had been reported in the newspapers, her youthful Majesty had suffered no personal loss; indeed, that this illustrious lady had nothing to do with the affair whatsoever. His client, an honest but simple-minded young lad, was of a singularly curious and prying disposition. Edward's visit to Buckingham Palace had only been prompted by his raging curiosity to see for himself what the royal residence looked like. In fact, the only difference between Edward and his learned friend Mr Bodkin, who had both been so keen to see the palace rooms for themselves, was that, whereas the Boy had been rambling about the palace by himself, Mr Bodkin had been placed under surveillance by some of the members of the royal household! With his extremely vivid imagination, the simple Boy had imagined a palace built of gold, silver, jasper and onyx. What ecstasy when he smeared himself with royal bear's grease from what he fancied was his Queen's own grease-pot. And what delight when he rolled on the royal bed and rubbed upon his person some authentic soot from the royal chimneys!

There was much laughter in court, even from Serjeant Adams and the magistrates. Mr Prendergast went on to describe the simple-minded Boy's desire to bring with him a few little things as mementoes of his visit to the Queen's palace. First he took some old worsted stockings, which he imagined to have been worn by his youthful sovereign. Then he saw the worthless coins, which he fancied also belonged to her Majesty. Only fancy what priceless relics these might be! And what about the 'Sword of State' he had found? These experiences went to the poor boy's head, and he began to imagine that he had been born in the palace and spent his entire life in there. In his own opinion, he had become one of the most exalted persons in the kingdom: nobody would any longer think of the exploits of the Duke of Wellington and Napoleon Bonaparte, or even the very war in Canada, but the whole public attention would be centred in himself. And indeed, the talk in town in recent days had been very much along the lines of 'Has anything further been heard about the boy discovered in the palace?' The spiteful, narrow-minded Board of Green Cloth had turned 'yellow' and decided to prosecute this poor boy for his prank, since he had anointed himself with the bear's fat of royalty, but Mr Prendergast hoped it would all end as it had started: as a great joke. He felt confident that the jury would look at this affair in its reasonable and fair light.

His job nearly done, Mr Prendergast sat down. He had a few witnesses of his own to call, first of whom was Edward's long-suffering employer, the respectable builder Mr Griffiths. The Boy had been a good and reliable worker, he said. He was very clever, but of a proud and ambitious turn of mind, never thinking anything good enough for him. When Edward had told him about his great ambition to see the inside of Buckingham Palace, Mr Griffiths had warned him against such an indiscretion. The Boy had been very fond of reading works of fancy and could sit up all night studying the *Globe* and *Sun* newspapers.

'But do you really call those works of fancy?' interjected the Chairman.

'No, not quite.'

'To my mind, the *Globe* and *Sun* are full of imagination!' said the irrepressible Mr Prendergast and there were again roars of laughter.

When asked by one of the jurors, Mr Griffiths confirmed that neither he nor his wife were related to the Boy. He also confirmed that he would be pleased to take Edward back into his employ. Another respectable London tradesman, Mr William Read, who had known Edward from birth, gave him an excellent character.

In his summing up, the Chairman commented that in a country not noted for its imaginary powers, this was certainly one of the most singular and extraordinary cases that had ever come before a court of justice. He went through the details of the case, giving the jury a clear hint as to his opinion when declaring that there did not appear to have been the least intention on the part of the boy to enter the palace for the purpose of theft. The act had been one of daring folly, and he hoped it would never be repeated. The jury accordingly returned a verdict of Not Guilty.

To end this remarkable trial, Serjeant Adams turned to Edward and said that he perfectly agreed with the verdict. The fact that the Boy had successfully entered Buckingham Palace without being impeded indicated that he possessed superior talents, which could elevate him to a much higher situation in life if they were properly directed. Edward politely bowed to the bonhomous Judge and said, 'Thank you, Sir,' before leaving the dock to join his master, Mr Griffiths.

The outcome of the trial of Edward Jones was widely reported in the newspapers.[19] A writer in the *John Bull* thought the proceedings most hilarious, particularly 'the story of the bad sovereign, the worsted stockings, and the dirty pot of bear's grease'. The *Examiner* did not agree in the slightest. Clearly, the Quarter Sessions had been utterly wrong to acquit such a lying scoundrel without reproaching him in the slightest: 'Not one word did the learned Judge utter in rebuke of the boy's lying, though he could not forego the opportunity of admiring his abilities. How the capacity of a Munchausen would be prized by Mr Serjeant Adams!'

The humorous and satirical newspapers of London naturally made the most of the scandal. With heavy-handed wit, *Figaro in London* speculated whether the 'Sweep in the Palace' was one of the bishops in disguise, carrying on an affair with one of the royal kitchen maids, or if the 'Sooty Gentleman' was in fact a protégé of Queen Victoria's mother, the Duchess of Kent, 'whose partiality for *sweeping* measures has made her the terror of all conservatives'. The truth might be that there were so many dirty characters at court that 'any one as comparatively unsullied as a sweep might remain for ever without fear of discovery'.[20]

The *Satirist*, another of these 'funny' newspapers, published the 'Suppressed Evidence of the Palace Spy'.[21] Edward Jones had climbed up and down the flues for some considerable period of time, it was alleged, and he had been eavesdropping on the conversations going on in bedrooms and chambers of state. The Queen and Prime Minister Lord Melbourne had been so hilarious that the Boy was 'fit to burst in the chimney all the while.' The crowning touch came when Queen Victoria's old governess promised her that 'if she was a good girl, she should soon have a German husband, which her uncle Leopold would provide for her. Her Majesty said as how she warn't in no sich a hurry, only she should like to get a good un when she did have one'.

In a later issue, the *Satirist* reported that 'the detection of the boy in Buckingham Palace has led to a regulation by which every tradesman having to do with repairs in the palace becomes accountable for those whom he employs. Does this, we wonder, apply to *cabinet-makers*?'[22] On a more serious note, Mr Griffiths was praised for his loyalty to the Boy. In an interview with another paper, the bonhomous builder declared that 'he had no doubt the Boy was cured of his inclination to visit the residence of royalty'.[23] The reader of this book can assess how right he was in this assumption through comparing the number of pages read thus far with the number of pages remaining …

2

The Boy Jones Strikes Again

You have heard of the chap that they found t'other day
In Buckingham Palace, I can tell you the truth –
'Twas in the next chamber to where the Queen lay,
They found me, this very identical youth.
At first, they all thought I had come there to plunder,
But I had no notion of stealing, not I –
Pages, nurses, and officers, pulled me from under
The very identical couch where she lay.

James Catnach, *The Boy that was found in the Palace*

It turned out that Mr Griffiths was as good as his word, taking Edward Jones back into his employ as a builder's boy. For a number of months, Edward did his work in good order, and was able to contribute to the family finances. Attracted by the newspaper publicity, quite a few people came to see the palace intruder as a curiosity, tipping Henry Jones a shilling or two for the privilege of being introduced to his notorious son. According to a newspaper story, one of them was Fenimore Cooper, the celebrated American novelist of *Last of the Mohicans* fame, who was in London at the time. He called on Henry Jones at his tailor's shop, suggesting that such a sharp, enterprising lad would have a brilliant future in America. Indeed, Cooper was himself willing to take Edward with him across the Atlantic to make his fortune. Since Henry Jones was not unwilling to let his son go to the United States, he arranged for Fenimore Cooper to meet Edward. Hoping to see a bright, active boy, the American was appalled to find 'a dull, undersized runt, remarkable only for his taciturnity and obstinacy', as a newspaper expressed it.[1] When asked whether he wanted to travel to the United States, the Boy declared that he would not go there under any circumstances, and Fenimore Cooper took no further interest in the matter. Shortly after the American's departure, the Joneses were visited by the stage-manager of one of the minor theatres. They were planning to stage the comedy *Intrusion; or a Guest Uninvited*, based on Edward Jones's exploits at the palace, and he thought it would be hilarious if the real-life intruder would be present to make his bow to the audience each night. This time, Edward was willing to take part, since he was offered liberal terms, but since Henry Jones was fearful his son would be put out to ridicule, he turned the offer down.

It is sad but true once more having to relate that hard work and long hours did not agree with the Boy: he was fired by the long-suffering Mr Griffiths for a second time later in 1839. In 1840, he was employed as an errand-boy by Mr Kendall, an apothecary practising in the Broadway, Westminster, but his lack of punctuality and industry once more earned him the sack. For several months, Edward was lounging about Bell-yard, doing very little work. When he felt like it, which was not particularly often, he helped old Henry Jones in his tailor's business. Sometimes, Edward absented himself for several days before returning without divulging where he had been. He could sleep all day and stay up all night. He was a very ugly boy and made it a habit never to have a bath or even wash his face; as a result, his appearance became so sinister that his father doubted whether any person would ever employ him again. A sullen, morose presence, he hardly spoke to his brothers and sister and was often at loggerheads with his father.

Poor Henry Jones himself was still very hard up, since the five guineas he had borrowed for Edward's defence was an immense sum for him. His main pleasure in life seems to have been to drink beer, and if his arithmetic ability allowed it, it must have displeased him immensely that the defence of his ungrateful, grubby son had cost him the equivalent of 1,260 pints of good London ale.

There was a communal groan from all Queen Victoria's admirers when she decided, in October 1839, to marry her first cousin, Prince Albert of Saxe-Coburg and Gotha. Many patriotic Britons doubted whether it was really right that England's Queen had to marry a foreigner. The radical *Charter* newspaper claimed to possess a list of eligible English bachelors to rival this foreign usurper.[2] In particular, Germans were considered quite greedy and avaricious: why support a German prince from the public purse when jobless Englishmen were grinding their teeth in the workhouse? It was feared that Prince Albert would bring with him a horde of money-grubbing parasites who would be added to the civil list and installed in comfortable apartments at the royal castles. In a letter, Charles Dickens made fun of 'German Sassages, fresh as imported from Saxe-Humbug and Go-to-her'! A popular street poem even contained the following deplorable verses:

Here I am in rags
From the land of all dirt,
To marry England's Queen,
And my name is Prince Albert.[3]

But still, Queen Victoria's marriage to Prince Albert in February 1840 was a great success. Although prevented by Parliament from playing any political role, the handsome, steady and industrious young Prince soon became quite popular. Both Prince Albert and Queen Victoria were monogamous by nature; as a result, their marriage was very happy. Their first child, Victoria, the Princess Royal, was born in November 1840; many more children were to come. Queen Victoria's relations with her mother, the intriguing and unpopular Duchess of Kent, had always been problematic. Although the Duchess was allowed apartments at Buckingham Palace, Victoria dismissed her mother's private secretary (and probable lover), the Irish adventurer Sir John Conroy. A more benign influence on the young Queen had been her governess, Baroness Louise Lehzen. Victoria was very fond of this formidable German lady, and although the Baroness had no formal position, she enjoyed much influence at court, including the supervision of the royal nursery. Albert used to refer to her as 'the House Dragon' and considered her wholly unfit to run a nursery, but since Victoria did not budge, the fierce Baroness kept her position at court.[4]

For her political education, Queen Victoria owed much to her adviser and friend William Lamb, 2nd Viscount Melbourne, who had been Whig Prime Minister since 1835. A father figure to the orphaned young Queen, he had helped her break free from the influence of her mother and Conroy. In the so-called Bedchamber Crisis of May 1839, Lord Melbourne resigned, and the Tory leader Sir Robert Peel was offered to form a government, although the Tories were in a minority in the House of Commons. Peel felt he needed a sign of confidence from the Queen. He knew that, during her long familiarity with Lord Melbourne, many court positions had been filled by the wives and daughters of senior Whigs, and he unwisely asked the Queen to dismiss some of her coterie. This, Victoria refused to do, although the Duke of Wellington tried to intervene. As a result, Peel refused to form a government, and Lord Melbourne returned to power.

On 9 June 1840, Prince Albert and Queen Victoria left Buckingham Palace in a low open carriage pulled by four horses. There were two outriders but no other attendants. Suddenly, a young man fired two pistols at the Queen and Prince. No one was hurt and the carriage drove on. A witness soon overpowered the diminutive would-be assassin and took his pistols away. He was found to be Edward Oxford, an eighteen-year-old tavern pot-boy who had vague republican notions and did not think it right England should be governed by a woman. Papers were found in his lodgings indicating that he belonged to a secret society called Young England, but the police found no evidence that this organisation existed outside Oxford's vivid imagination. Of more interest were some references to important communications from Hanover, raising the possibility that Victoria's wicked uncle, Ernest, Duke of Cumberland and King of Hanover, might have employed Oxford as an assassin to get her out of the way and secure his own rights to the throne before she had any offspring. In the end, the police were convinced that Oxford had acted alone; he was found guilty but insane and put into Bedlam.[5] Although there was outrage in the press that any lunatic with a brace of pistols could come so very close to shooting the Queen of England, it does not appear that any significant improvements were made to royal security, nor to the guarding of Buckingham Palace.

At half past one in the morning of 3 December 1840, all seemed well at Buckingham Palace. Mrs Lilly, the Queen's midwife, was one of the few people awake, since she was looking after the Princess Royal, who was just two weeks old. To facilitate her work, the midwife's own bed was situated in the nursery of the infant princess, near the Queen's bedroom and dressing room. But just as she was going to sleep, Mrs Lilly heard the creaking of a door. There should be no one about this time of night. The suspicious midwife crawled out of bed, opened the nursery door and called out, 'Who's there?' No person answered this challenge, but the startled Mrs Lilly saw that the door of the Queen's dressing room was slowly opened by some person inside that room. The midwife repeated her challenge, but the only result was that the door was suddenly slammed shut from the inside.

Mrs Lilly acted with commendable resolution. She bolted the door from her side and rang the bell to summon aid. Kinnaird, one of the Queen's pages, promptly came to her assistance. He was accompanied by no less a personage than Baroness Lehzen, Queen Victoria's redoubtable former governess. Together, the Baroness, the midwife and the page cautiously unbolted the door and entered the dressing room. They searched the room for a while, without finding anything untoward. But when the craven Kinnaird looked under the Queen's sofa, he hastily backed away without a word, looking like if he had seen a ghost. Had the two ladies been characters in *The Mysteries of Udolpho*, this sinister nocturnal escapade would have sent them into hysterics, but Mrs Lilly and the Baroness were made of sterner stuff than Mrs Radcliffe's lachrymose heroines. After Baroness Lehzen had resolutely shoved the sofa out of the way, the midwife's brawny hand collared an ugly, stunted boy who had hidden underneath it. He grinned at them with his wide mouth but made no attempt to escape.[6]

A patrol of the Buckingham Palace police swiftly appeared on the scene and took the boy into custody. There was general alarm and consternation when one of the constables discovered that they were actually dealing with the same strange character who had broken into the palace back in December 1838. Although nearly two years had gone by, the unprepossessing features of Edward Jones had not changed much. When asked what he had seen from his hiding place, he smirked knowingly but kept stubbornly silent. Neither Mrs Lilly nor Baroness Lehzen had made an outcry when Edward was arrested, and the police constables had swiftly dragged him downstairs, in order not to alarm the Queen, who was in bed just one door away.

In the morning, when Edward Jones was in custody at the Gardener's-lane station house, the authorities were facing two difficult decisions. Firstly, how should Queen Victoria be told that a boy had been hiding in her dressing room; secondly, what was to be done with Edward Jones. The first of these quandaries was solved simply through deferring the decision to Prince Albert. After he had been fully informed about the outrage, the Prince decided to inform Queen Victoria himself.

As the Queen herself expressed it in her Journal,

> Albert told me, that he had just heard, when he got up, that a man had been found, under the sofa in my sitting room. Mrs Lilly then told me that at ½ past 1, she heard the creaking of the door from my room, & called several times to know who was there, but got no answer. The door went on opening, & when she, at last, called out again, it closed & she jumped up, & bolted the door. She ran out, called Lehzen, & they sent for Kinnaird (one of my Pages) watching the door. The Audience Room, & Lehzen's were searched 1st & then mine, Kinnaird, looking under the corner of the sofa on which I had been rolled into the Bedroom but said nothing. Lehzen however, pushed it away, & there on the ground, lay a lad who was seized & would not speak but he was quite unarmed. After he had been taken downstairs, he said he had meant no harm, & had only come to see the Queen! We have since heard that he was in the Palace once before, & was ½ witted, & had merely come out of curiosity. But supposing he had come into the Bedroom, how frightened I should have been. Mrs Lilly showed the greatest presence of mind, & so did my dear Lehzen.[7]

When the Privy Council assembled on Friday 4 December, they probably echoed their Monarch's grateful remarks concerning Baroness Lehzen and Mrs Lilly. But for the valiant and decisive conduct of these two ladies, Edward Jones's ambition to meet the Queen might well have been fulfilled, under the most ludicrous circumstances. What if he had sneaked into the Queen's bedroom, pulled her bedclothes off and yelled 'View hallo!' And what if he had gone into the nursery, stolen the infant Princess, and run off with her? And how long had the boy been hidden underneath the sofa in the Queen's dressing room, and what had he seen and heard during this time?

After some deliberation, it was decided to take the highly unusual and controversial course of examining Edward Jones at the Home Office, and letting the Privy Council sentence him. There may well have been several causes for this archaic machinery being resurrected to deal with the Boy Jones. Trial by the Privy Council as a prerogative court had been used in the Middle Ages down to Tudor times to deal with powerful barons suspected of treason, magnates who would be out of the reach of ordinary courts for reasons of wealth and influence. So why treat the Boy Jones as if he had been the Earl of Essex in the time of Queen Elizabeth I? Well, firstly, as we know, the 1838 trial had been turned into a complete farce by Mr Prendergast, to the embarrassment of the Buckingham Palace officials. Since this time, the Boy had stolen nothing and no weapon had been found upon him, a charge of burglary would surely fail, and Jones's barrister would have a field-day mocking the Queen's bungling guardians, who had been led such a merry dance by young Jones, and exposing the government to ridicule and resentment in the press. By late 1840, Lord Melbourne had been Prime Minister for six years, and his Whig government was becoming unpopular. The Boy Jones affair could prove potentially very damaging, since it could be construed as proof that the government was failing to protect the Queen; thus, it was important for Lord Melbourne's ministry to suppress it. Before the Privy Council, Jones would not be allowed any kind of legal representation. Secondly, it seemed highly likely that Jones had spent the better part of the night concealed underneath the sofa in the Queen's dressing room, where he would have been in a position to observe many things. What if he told some scandalous story, true or false, about seeing the Queen in a state of nudity, or gave salacious details of her evening-time tête-à-tête with Prince Albert? Such things simply could not be allowed, whatever means had to be taken to avoid them. Before the Privy Council, the Boy Jones would not be able to say very much, and there would be no journalists to report his utterances.[8]

News of the outrage at Buckingham Palace spread like wildfire. At first, it was not generally believed, but after it transpired that the Boy would actually be taken to the Home Office, there was immense interest among both high and low. Several newspaper reporters paid a call at the station house to see the prisoner. They elicited the information that he was indeed the same miscreant who had entered the palace back in 1838. Their opinion about his personal attractions remained uniformly unflattering. *The Times* described him as a 'dirty, ill-looking fellow'; *The Morning Chronicle* thought him 'very short for his age, and very meanly dressed, with a most repulsive appearance'; the jolly *Satirist* likened him to the Black Prince since he was so very dirty and yet had sat on the throne![9] Nevertheless, the Boy affected an air of great consequence, haughtily requesting the police constables to address him in a more becoming manner. At twelve o'clock, he was taken to the Home Office in a cab, to face the Privy Council, namely the Marquess of Normanby, Home Secretary, the Earl of Uxbridge, Lord Chamberlain, the Earl of Errol, Lord Steward, and Viscount Duncannon, Lord Privy Seal. The Hon. Charles Augustus Murray, whose sword had been stolen by Edward back in 1838, and who had since advanced to become Comptroller of the Household, also attended. So did Mr Fox Maule, Under-Secretary of State, Mr Hall, the Chief Magistrate of Bow Street, and Colonel Rowan, the Commissioner of Police.

Far from being overawed by this noble and distinguished company, Edward Jones freely told them that, on Monday night, he had scaled the wall of Buckingham Palace Gardens, halfway up Constitution Hill. Without being detected, he had strolled up to the palace and entered through a window. He was hungry and searched for food, but many people were moving about, and he prudently crept out the same way he had entered, thinking it too unsafe to stay the night. Having gone home to fortify himself with a meal, he returned the next day at nine in the evening, again scaled the wall at Constitution Hill, sneaked past the soldiers on duty, and entered the palace through a window in the servants' quarters. He freely roamed the rooms below stairs, before going to sleep under the bed of one of the servants. On Wednesday evening, he emerged from his hiding place and helped himself to some soup and other edibles from the kitchen, before walking up the servants' stairs and entering the sumptuously decorated Green Drawing Room, which served as a huge ante-room to the Throne Room. Having spent some time admiring this elegant room, he proceeded to the Throne Room itself, sat on the throne and handled various ornaments and pieces of furniture. Edward Jones then proceeded to the Queen's private apartments, having a good look round before hiding in the dressing room, where he had probably spent several hours lurking underneath the sofa.

After Edward had freely offered to point out to the authorities exactly where he had entered the palace, their Lordships directed the police to take the Boy Jones back to the scene of the crime. At two in the afternoon, the Boy was taken back to the Home Office to face a further grilling. When asked whether he had seen the Queen or the Princess Royal, he answered in the negative, although he thought he had heard a noise coming from her Majesty's room.

Poor Henry Jones, who had also been summoned, was severely scolded by their Lordships for failing to control his errant son. The timorous old man told the Council that he believed his unfortunate son was not of sound mind. Since Edward had always found it difficult to gain and keep paid employment, old Jones had been surprised when, on Monday, Edward had told him that he had obtained another place, and was going to it that evening. Dr Fisher, of Argyle-street, physician of the 'A' division of police, and Mr Davies, surgeon, of King-street, were of the opinion that, although the prisoner's head 'was of a most peculiar formation', they could not give any decided opinion concerning his sanity or lack of it. The page Kinneard testified that when the Boy Jones was led out of Buckingham Palace, he had said that he had wanted to see what was going on in the palace, that he might write about it. If he were discovered, he had reasoned, he would be as well off as Edward Oxford, who had shot at the Queen, since Oxford fared better in Bedlam than he himself did out of it. During the entire inquiry, the prisoner never once looked up, but kept his eyes fixed on the ground.

The verdict of the Privy Council was that, since no stolen property or dangerous weapon had been found on the Boy, the best thing was to inflict a summary punishment. A warrant was duly made out and signed by Mr Hall, committing the prisoner to three months hard labour in the House of Corrections, Tothill-street, as a rogue and vagabond. Edward was immediately afterwards led out into a waiting cab, to avoid any inquisitive journalists.[10]

Lord Normanby ordered Viscount Duncannon, the Lord Privy Seal, to investigate how much Edward's story about his three-day residence in Buckingham Palace could be relied upon. Could security really have been that lax? In a letter to the Prime Minister Lord Melbourne, Lord Duncannon retold the Boy's own story about his wanderings, with the added comment that, unfortunately, a great part of what he had said was definitely true. Lord Duncannon had retraced the Boy's steps, finding telltale signs that he had indeed entered the palace through a lower-ground-floor window, with the greatest of ease. Although every window had a bolt and every shutter a bar, the slack royal servants had not made use of them. An under-butler stoutly maintained that the back door communicating with the servants' hall had been securely locked by himself, but from the Boy's description of his wanderings, Lord Duncannon had no doubt this measure had been forgotten. There were marks of soot on the throne, and dirty fingermarks on a bowl of soup in the servant's kitchen. It was a disgrace that the Queen's London residence was not more strictly guarded, Lord Duncannon pontificated. But for the presence of mind of the nurse, her Majesty would have been dreadfully alarmed. There should be somebody about at night, and the Queen's apartment should really be cut off from the rest of the palace when the pages went to bed.[11]

Lord Normanby made sure that a short news communiqué was given to the press, containing the basic facts about the examination of the Boy Jones in front of the Privy Council. There was no mention of the Boy stealing food in the kitchen, visiting the Green Drawing Room or sitting on the throne, and it was asserted that he had not seen or heard either the Queen or the Princess Royal. The enterprising London journalists were not convinced, however. Why, if there were no tasty scandal to hide, had the Boy been treated as if he had been some great magnate accused of treason, back in the old Star Chamber days? Inquiries at the Home Office were fruitless, and Buckingham Palace provided only the brief statement that neither the Queen nor the infant princess had suffered any ill effect from this extraordinary midnight visit to the palace. Nor did the police have any juicy titbits to pass on to them: they merely said that they were under strict orders not to say a word about the palace intruder. It was supposed that while the Boy Jones was in prison, the law officers of the Crown would be consulted as to whether it was appropriate to indict the Boy for secreting himself in the palace for the purpose of committing a felony.

Since there was immense curiosity about the Boy Jones among the Londoners, the journalists followed every possible lead about the mystery boy in the palace. They managed to find out the identity of the boy's father, 'a poor but industrious man, living at No. 16, Bell-yard, York-street, Westminster, and who obtains a scanty livelihood by working as a tailor in a shed in Darby-street, Cannon-row.' When they tracked down Henry Jones at his shabby little tailor's shop, his reply to all enquiries was 'I am requested by a high authority not to answer any questions'. Who this high authority was he would not say.[12]

But the journalists did not give up. They found out, probably through greasing the palm of one of the turnkeys, that in Tothill-fields, the Boy was talking freely about his experiences. He had sat on the throne, seen the Queen, and heard the Princess Royal squall, as he expressed it. He had entered the palace by climbing down a chimney, he asserted. When he came off the treadmill for the first time, the turnkey asked him how he had liked it. The Boy grinned and commented that if he had done the crime, he must accept the punishment. Edward was much less pleased with the thin gruel and stale bread served to the inmates of this dismal prison, however.

The newspapers avidly published any little titbit about the Boy Jones, the media celebrity of the day. According to *The Times*, 'The subject engrosses public attention at the west end of town. Nothing else is talked of, and the general opinion is that some further punishment than confinement for three months ought to be inflicted, to prevent another such an unpleasant, and might be dangerous, intrusion into the Royal Palace.' The Lord Steward and the Lord Chamberlain were undertaking an official investigation of the case, and the bumbling royal servants could look forward to 'a rigid examination' about their negligence. There was eventually a 'leak' that many circumstances spoke in favour of the Boy's version that he had stayed in the palace for three days, including the telltale fingermarks in the 'stock for soup'. The Boy's shoes had been found in one of the ground-floor rooms. The sofa he had hidden under was a most costly and magnificent piece of furniture, ordered specially for the accommodation of the royal and illustrious visitors who call to pay their respects to the Queen. On 6 December, a party of magistrates went to Tothill-fields to question the Boy. Edward freely told them that he had gone into Buckingham Palace for the purpose of writing a book, since he thought a description of the arrangement of the chambers, and the doings of the people inhabiting them, would interest many people, in particular 'the dressing room of her Majesty' and what went on in there.[13]

There were several handbills and catchpenny prints celebrating the exploits of the Boy Jones. Of these, the amazingly titled 'A Stranger in Her Majesty's Bedroom!', reproduced as an illustration in this book, has a claim to precedence. Jemmy Catnach, the kingpin of London's ballad trade, issued a street ballad of his own, 'The Boy that was found in the Palace', of which the first verse served as an epigraph to this chapter; the second one is to follow:

Prince Albert, you all know, is in a decline, sirs,
And the young Queen must look out again, it is clear –
So I wanted to ask her if she would be mine, sirs,
I should like the identical thousands a-year.
Now what do you think, just to shorten my tail, sirs,
They called me a madman, and what is worse still,
For my second appearance refused to take bail,
But sent me to tread the identical mill.[14]

The *Satirist* was a controversial 'funny' newspaper of the time. It was run by a certain Barnard Gregory, who had a profitable sideline in blackmailing: he threatened to publish various scandalous news stories about wealthy people unless the 'victim' paid to have them suppressed. The *Satirist* journalists specialised in satirical retellings of the scandalous news of the day, with some spicy puns and poems added according to the fashion of the time. Lampooning the Queen and her court was considered particularly amusing. As we know, the *Satirist* had published a squib on the Boy Jones already back in 1838, but from December 1840 onward, the Boy and his real and fictitious adventures would become a recurrent feature in this lewd and disreputable newspaper.

As could be expected, the 13 December issue of the *Satirist* was full of the Boy Jones.[15] In a long article, every aspect of 'The Sweep's Visit to Buckingham Palace' is thoroughly debated. Was the Boy Jones the agent of the Duke of Cumberland, on a mission to steal away the Princess Royal? Or perhaps he was motivated by some strange grudge against royalty, as Hamlet would put it,

As swift as meditation, or the thoughts of love
To *sweep* to his revenge ...

The narrow escape of the Queen from meeting the sweep face to face was also discussed in prose and verse; substituting the royal wet-nurse Mrs Packer for her colleague Mrs Lilly, they have the Queen exclaim,

Behold me – from a wretch
Than Satan blacker
Just saved by Providence,
And Mrs Packer!

Her Majesty is less amused by the newspaper reports of the Boy Jones's 'aural experience of the Princess Royal's singular capacity and tendency to squall', however:

'Squall', she exclaimed, almost hysterically, when the young Chatelar of the flue's expression was repeated to her by the Lady in Waiting. 'Squall! just like the common children! When were the issue of *Royal* parents ever known to squall, I should like to know? The boy is a monster, a perfect cacodemon.'

Another article tried to reconstruct the 'Dialogue between the Boy Jones and the Members of the Privy Council':

Examined by MELBOURNE – How was it, Master Jones, that you preferred entering the Palace by the window to any other way?

JONES – 'Cause, when I was in the Palace before, about a year ago, I was told 'never to darken the doors again'; so I chose the window, although it was more *pane*-ful to get in that way.

MELBOURNE – What did you do first, after you got in?

BOY – I tried if I could see anything of her Majesty.

MELBOURNE – And what were your intentions, sirrah?

BOY – Strictly honourable, of course.

The Boy then starts describing a series of scandalous incidents: Lord Melbourne giving directions to the cook about sending the dinner to the bakehouse, Prince Albert kissing one of the Maids of Honour, and Mrs Lilly fortifying herself with some swigs of cherry brandy before breastfeeding her young charge! Just when he is about to tell the Privy Council what he saw in the Queen's dressing room, they abruptly decide 'that for fear of more delicate disclosures, the boy should not be questioned further at present'. He was sent to prison, and

Now he in chains and in the prison garb is,
Mourning the crime that couples *Jones* with *darbies*.

3

Return of In-I-Go Jones

The 'sayings and doings' at Buckingham Palace
I would tell without favour, fear, falsehood or malice.
Did they dream by a treadmill my soul could be frightened,
And because I soared high as a jailbird be spited?
With my thumb at my nose, and my tongue in my cheek,
What care I for Home Office, lobster, or beak?
My loyal attentions they ne'er shall restrain,
To move in high circles I'd 'quod' it again;
And never say die, nor sing small with 'peccavi'
Hang their locks, and my cousin Jones's locker of Davy!

From *The Era* of 28 March 1841

On 2 March 1841, the Boy Jones was liberated from Tothill-fields Prison and handed over to his father. The latter was severely scolded by Mr Hall the magistrate and ordered to take every possible care of his delinquent son, to watch his actions closely, and not to spare the rod if there was any indiscretion. Henry Jones was appalled to see how pale, thin and careworn poor Edward looked after three months of hard labour on the treadmill, with very little to eat. On Mr Hall's insistence, he asked Edward how he had broken into Buckingham Palace, but the magistrate's hope that the presence of his father would induce Edward to be more truthful proved in vain. Although the Boy's body had been severely chastised, his spirit remained unbroken: he just whistled insolently and said, 'Oh, by the door, or window.' Mr Hall offered to provide Edward with employment as a seaman, but the truculent Boy was unwilling to go to sea, and Henry Jones knew that this feeling was fully shared by his wife, who was much looking forward to seeing her firstborn again. To end this dismal interview, the bullying Mr Hall delivered another volley of abuse at timid old Henry Jones for turning down a good offer and not letting his son go to sea without delay.[1]

Back home in Bell-yard, the Boy was welcomed by his doting mother, who had missed him very much. But did he reciprocate her love, or even respect her? If he did, he made a good job of hiding it, remaining as surly and uncommunicative as ever. Since every man, woman and child in Westminster knew who he was, he could hardly go outdoors without being mobbed. Quite a few people came to Bell-yard to see the Boy as a curiosity. Penniless old Henry Jones welcomed their tips, but the Boy remained as truculent as ever, hardly speaking a word to his distinguished visitors. Journalists were also sniffing about, hopeful of getting an interview with the Boy.[2] One of them could report that the great celebrity 'has from his infancy been fond of reading, but no one would form such an opinion from his personal appearance, which is anything but prepossessing. His countenance is exceedingly sullen; he is very diminutive for his age, which, we understand, is seventeen years.'[3] The only coherent utterance made by the Boy was that his only object in going into the palace had been to hear the conversation of the Queen and Prince Albert, so that he could write a book about them.

The newspapers kept publishing any snippet of news about the Boy Jones.[4] He tried to gain paid employment, but his recent notoriety barred every door. On Sunday 14 March, he attended a Methodist chapel twice and said he was determined to join a teetotal society. On Monday 15 March, Edward spent all day at home, but at eight in the evening, he told his father he wanted to attend a temperance meeting nearby. As had often happened before, he did not return home.

At half past one in the morning of Tuesday 16 March 1841, all seemed well at Buckingham Palace. After the Boy Jones's December visit, it had been arranged that a troop of fourteen police constables from the 'A' Division would guard the palace, with two sergeants in charge on alternate nights. On Tuesday night, Police Sergeant Glover was in command of this impromptu anti-Boy Jones police force. When he was patrolling the Picture Gallery, he heard a noise coming from one of the lobbies leading from the grand staircase into the Picture Gallery. When looking around, he saw a pair of dirty shoes on the floor and a person crouching in a recess nearby. Shining his lantern at this individual, he could see that it was a familiar figure, who he had seen before at the station house …

'What, Jones, is that you?' he called out.

'Yes, it's me,' the lad replied meekly.

Sergeant Clover saw that the Boy Jones had been eating cold meat and potatoes, which he had stolen in the royal kitchen and wrapped into his handkerchief. He collared the palace intruder and led him to the Gardener's-lane station house, where Inspector Hickman was on duty. When the Boy was asked how he had got into the palace, he insolently replied, 'The same way as before!' He had been in the palace all day, he asserted, but this was soon proven to be false, since his shoes were quite wet with mud. The Boy Jones was locked into one of the cells, charged with being found concealed in Buckingham Palace for an unlawful purpose.[5]

In the morning, when questioned by two police inspectors, the Boy was a little more communicative. He denied going into the palace for any felonious purpose; his plan had been to record the conversation of the Queen, Prince and courtiers, so that he could write a book and make his fortune. The inspectors were astounded when he began to describe his recent exploits. He had visited a room where there was a coronet and many precious jewels, all of which he had handled; he had again sat on the throne; he had visited a grand library and read some of the books in there. When the policemen doubted this latter statement, the Boy named the books and their positions on the shelves. He had once observed two servants in the process of lighting a fire; when one of them started to whistle, the other said, 'Jack, you know that is against the rules,' but the insolent fellow sullenly replied, 'There are many more rules that are broken in this house,' which the Boy found curious.

At one in the afternoon, the police inspectors took their prisoner to the Home Office, where he underwent a long and gruelling examination before the Privy Council. Mr Hall, the magistrate, was joined by the Marquess of Normanby, the Earl of Uxbridge, the Hon. Mr Murray, Mr Fox Maule and other officials. This time, there were no leaks to the press, and the proceedings were strictly secret. According to a journalist, 'Jones affects on the present occasion, as on the two previous, the greatest indifference, and refuses to give any answers.'[6] The only witness called was Sergeant Glover, who had taken the Boy into custody. Many newspaper journalists were waiting outside the Home Office, but all they were told by the gruff Mr Hall was that the prisoner had been committed to the House of Corrections, Tothill-fields, as a rogue and a vagabond, for a period of three months. Since 'the extraordinary circumstance of his having obtained a third entrance into Buckingham Palace formed the all-engrossing subject of conversation', the journalists tried their best to get hold of some further information. They went to see Henry Jones, but the broken old man had nothing to tell them except that he himself and his wife had just been summoned to Bow Street by Mr Hall, to be treated to another severe tongue-lashing for taking such bad care of their son.

Adopting the policy of locking the door after the horse had bolted, the Department of Woods and Forests was shaken out of its habitual inertia and devoted some of its time 'in ascertaining how such self presentment at Court was in future to be prevented'. After a long survey, they decided that all basement windows were to be secured by wrought iron bars, thus preventing ingress or egress by these means. Men were immediately set to work, and the job was completed by the end of March.[7] At about the same time, Sir J. McDonald of the War Office made a most careful assessment of all approaches and entrances to Buckingham Palace, both from public thoroughfares and from the gardens, the result of which was the appointment of three more sentries.[8]

Frustrated by the lack of reliable news, and unable to obtain any leaks from the Tothill-fields turnkeys, the journalists had to be content with idle speculation. The pro-Jones lobby was admiring the pluck of this young boy, who was single-handedly taking on the royal family, the government and the police. He was a harmless enthusiast, they claimed, and had no intention to harm the Queen or to steal any valuables from the palace. Indeed, the Queen should be grateful that her defective palace security was shown up by such a benign figure, rather than by some pistol-toting lunatic or assassin.

The anti-Jones press deplored that such a scoundrel would get only three months in prison, since this was the highest punishment for his offence; surely, he ought to be flogged up and down Constitution Hill for half an hour. They had to be content with announcing that Mr Hall had ordered that the punishment of hard labour had been added to the Boy's prison term. Although there were now fourteen policemen permanently posted to the palace, these bungling constables had been unable to prevent the Boy from entering the premises. The law was an ass, since simple trespass was not a criminal offence; how could the Boy be prevented from paying her Majesty Boy Jones in some way, by exporting him to some far-away place, but how could this be done when the government was showing the same blameworthy idleness as the police?

The jolly *Satirist* was up to its usual fun.[9] It had been reported that the meat eaten by the Boy Jones when he was arrested had been a cold leg of mutton, but instead it must be said that on a visit to the Queen, he had been presented with the *cold shoulder*. But what had the Boy had occasion to see in the royal larder? Perhaps there had been a large bowl of *pap* (porridge) to be consumed by the Princess Royal and the elderly Duke of Sussex, with an identical *spoon* for each? Or maybe 'a dish containing several large *German sausages*, which her Majesty had evidently sent away untouched; having, as may be conjectured, been already surfeited by that article?' Interestingly, it had been reported that the domestics at Buckingham Palace were gossiping that the Boy Jones was in the pay of the Duke of Cumberland, on a mission to steal away 'the Royal babby'. But although it was not unlikely that the demon duke would be delighted to steal the Royal infant and her mamma too, the journalist found it improbable that he would employ a shoeless urchin to aid him in such an intrigue.

The *Age* newspaper instead imagined some spurious correspondence between the key players in the Boy Jones drama, including a letter from Lord Melbourne to Prince Albert, allegedly written to ease the Prince's worries that the Boy had been up to no good with his wife:

MY DEAR PRINCE – Do not trouble your head about it. If it had been Tom Jones – you may, perhaps, have heard that there is an English author of the name of Fielding, who, considering he was only an Englishman, was almost as

clever as your Goethe – and our honoured Mistress, Lady Bellaston, or Molly
Seagrim, or Mrs. Waters – then there might have been something annoying in
the business. That is, if trifles of the kind can be considered annoying. If I had
found man, or boy, in my poor deceased Caroline's room – I should not have
deemed it necessary to say any thing about it. You, my dear Prince, are young,
but you will learn in time.   MELBOURNE

The reference to 'my poor deceased Caroline' is a sly reference to Lord
Melbourne's late wife Lady Caroline Lamb, whose many affairs, with Lord
Byron and others, he had tolerated.

Another letter purports to put the Boy Jones on the stage:

DEAR SIR – Don't you think the boy Jones would make an admirable
Melodrame. We are tired of Jack Shephard, Dick Turpin, Catherine Hayes,
and all the old ones. The 'Newgate Calendar' is used up – the Old Bailey
returns worked out. A new ground must be broken; and what can be better
than Jones? We have a Queen and a Court ready made – scenery, decorations,
property, all to match. Mr. Keeley would do the boy Jones. Dark moustaches,
dark lanthorn, dark eyes, dark deeds, dark sayings. Romantic feelings for the
Queen, performed by Miss Ellen Tree, who rejects his offers ...[10]

A *Weekly Chronicle* journalist outdid all his colleagues by publishing a long
interview with Henry Jones, containing everything he thought his readers
would want to know about the extraordinary exploits of 'the Queen's
Visitor'.[11] Since an early age, young Edward Jones had been a very restless,
inquisitive spirit, this journalist claimed, always thirsting for information.
He had been sent to school early and achieved a high degree of proficiency
in reading, penmanship and arithmetic, before leaving school when he was
nearly twelve years old. He became errand-boy to an apothecary in the
Strand for six months, and to another in the Broadway where he lasted
eight months before being asked to leave because of 'restlessness'. Having
spent several months musing and scheming 'how to get on in the world', he
decided that he wanted to become an architect. To put his foot on the first
rung on the ladder to achieving this lofty goal, he became a builder's boy at
Mr Griffiths' yard in Coventry-street. Henry Jones told the journalist that
he and his wife had not known about Edward being missing until they went
to the builder's yard with fresh linen for their son and were told that he
had run away.[12] After a week, they had been fearful Edward had destroyed
himself, but then they saw the newspaper articles about the Sweep in the
Palace and suspected this individual was their absconded son. Poor Henry
Jones ruined himself to raise the five guineas to pay for a solicitor to watch
proceedings and council to defend Edward. But still, his son showed him no
gratitude. Edward believed that 'he was born in a sphere far below what he

considered his rightful rank in the scale of humanity' and frequently said that his father's hovel was not good enough for him. He lost his job with Mr Griffiths 'on account of his affairs getting embarrassed' and could not get another one since he 'had a thorough aversion to manual labour'.

After becoming unemployed, Edward wanted to invent a new kind of ink and a novel form of steel pen, but although he invested every penny he got from running errands and looking after horses to purchase equipment, 'all his speculations were unfortunate'. Frustrated and down-spirited, he decided to make one final attempt to distinguish himself, by again entering Buckingham Palace to collect material for a book about the sayings and doings at the palace. That plan came to nothing, and the Boy was imprisoned with hard labour and low diet: when he got out of jail, his mother was shocked to see that he was only the skeleton of the boy he had once been. At this time, things were as bad as ever with the Jones family: in their hovel, there were no beds, and they slept on miserable rags; all their furniture was worth just a few shillings.

The journalist, who had probably visited Bell-yard before the Boy's third visit to Buckingham Palace, wrote that Edward's appearance was 'the reverse of prepossessing'. He was pale, ugly and pock-marked, but orderly and clean in dress; his shoes shone with beeswax, which he used in want of polish. He was humane and kind-hearted, his parents claimed, and once defended a weaker boy against a strong one. When tea was put on the table, Edward showed a great degree of orderliness: he took upon himself to rearrange the contents of the tray until he thought everything was in the perfect position. In contrast, when going to bed, he threw all his wearing apparel in a heap on the floor. His constant talk was of writing a book about Buckingham Palace and its inhabitants. Edward wrote both prose and poetry, his father asserted, and he could sit for hours revising and correcting his work, before finally throwing it on the fire; 'none of his effusions were ever seen by his father or any one in the house.'

One week after being released from prison, the journalist claimed, Edward had called on Mr Hall the magistrate, asking for employment, but the only result of this was that Henry Jones was sent for and upbraided for not getting his son away. No step was taken to deter the Boy from returning to Buckingham Palace, Henry Jones asserted, and the gruelling work on the treadmill had not taken away his limitless curiosity. Having entered Buckingham Palace for a third time, he was soon arrested again. He had once more sat on the throne, and handled books in a grand library, and seen the coronet and jewels in another room. The journalist was most indignant about the archaic way the Boy had been tried, after the old Star Chamber fashion: 'This may possibly be according to law, but it is certainly very much at variance with justice; and whatever power Mr Hall, the chief magistrate at Bow Street, may have to adjudicate secretly in this *antique* manner, the sooner he abstains from using it the better.' The behaviour of the unfortunate Boy Jones before the Privy Council had been that of a person who is utterly dejected and cares little of what happens to him. His grieving mother was fearful he would starve to death if imprisoned for more than three months.

On 21 March, a letter signed 'Henry Jones, 16 Bell-yard, York-street, Westminster' but probably written by some anti-Melbourne journalist who had interviewed the old man, appeared in the *Standard* newspaper.[13] The Boy Jones had for some time 'possessed an insane idea of intruding himself into Buckingham Palace, in order to learn about the sayings and doings of the Court'. After his first offence, he had been tried and acquitted by an honest English jury. But after his second intrusion, the underlings of the palace had been frightened that their own indiscretions would become public knowledge, and they 'had adopted the novel and un-English mode of trying him by a secret court, where he was not allowed either access to his friends, or the assistance of counsel'. Sentenced without a trial, the Boy had endured three months in a horrible Bastille: 'When he came out of prison, on the second of this month, he was as thin as a skeleton, and obviously sinking under the effects of overwork and under-diet.' Mr Hall had offered to send the Boy away on a ship of war, and later to get him a situation somewhere in the colonies, but his proposal had seemed excessively harsh to the Joneses, so Mr Hall upbraided them for changing their minds, and told them to go away.

After his first period of imprisonment, the Boy had tried to look for work, but no one wanted to employ such a notorious figure. On 8 March, he had said, 'Father, I find here everyone says "That's the boy that was in the Palace" – and no body will employ me. I will go to Mr Hall and beg him to get me sent to sea or somewhere.' But his audience with the short-tempered magistrate did not have the desired effect; for some reason, Henry Jones had been sent for and 'talked to in a very rough manner' before both father and son were summarily dismissed. After the Boy's third visit to the palace, the Joneses had been shamefully treated. After a police officer had informed them that their son was in custody, they had gone to Bow Street, where they were told to sit in a waiting room. After humbly waiting for an hour and a half, Henry Jones went out to ask if he might see his son. The answer was no, since Edward had been taken to the Home Office. The reason the Joneses had not been told, an official explained, was that they might have 'made a noise in the street'. At the Home Office, they were denied entrance by some angry constables, and after waiting outside for two hours they went home. The next thing they heard about poor Edward was that he had again been convicted by the same secret court, and that he was back in prison to be killed by inches through under-diet and overwork.

4

The Boy Jones Finds Himself Famous

Hush, hush, royal darling,
Pray cease thy sad moans;
For far, far away
Is naughty young Jones!

From *A Peep into the Palace*, by 'E. Jones'

After his first intrusion into Buckingham Palace, the Boy Jones had become something of a 'B'-list celebrity; his second strike had taken him to the 'A' list and his third catapulted him into becoming a media superstar. The biographer of street ballad kingpin Jemmy Catnach wrote that, all of a sudden, the people of England had a burning desire to know more about the Boy who had three times entered Buckingham Palace.[1] Just like Lord Byron, the Boy Jones had woken up one day to find himself famous. But unlike the publicity-seeking poetical peer, the Boy Jones found his fame very irksome. People pointed him out in the streets and made various facetious remarks; he could go nowhere without being followed by a gang of local guttersnipes who were calling out, 'There is the boy who went into the Palace!'

The Boy Jones was 'written up – and down – by ballad-mongers, newspapers and magazine contributors'. The Bloomsbury print and ballad seller E. Lloyd issued a vast quantity of ballads, squibs and cartoons for street sale, with titles like 'Her Majesty's Chimney sweep', 'The Royal Sooter', 'The Buckingham Palace Hero' and 'The Royal Flue Faker'. Henry Mayhew once spoke to a 'patterer', a street seller of books and pamphlets about sensational recent affairs, who gathered a crowd around him by giving a lively or horrible description of the papers or books they were 'working'. This worthy told him that 'The boy Jones in the Palace wasn't much more of an affair for the running patterer; the ballad-singers – or street-screamers, as we calls 'em – had the pull out of that. The patter wouldn't take; they had heard it all in the newspapers before. ... There is nothing beats a stunning good murder after all.'[2]

The musician James Bruton wrote a comic song about the Boy Jones, entitled 'The Boy wot visits the Palace' and containing stanzas like this:

He is a fool, and dull in look,
And yet he wants to 'write a book!'
But why at this should wonder be?
There's greater fools wrote books that he!

From conversation he could glean,
That took place twixt the Prince and Queen,
The fact he learnt, to give us joy,
Their next baby is to be a boy!

Into the Pantry did he stroll,
The mutton of the Queen he stole,
And while he was inclin'd to cram,
'Tis well he didn't take her *Lamb*.

Some say 'twill be his future plan,
To set up for a Gentleman;
His town-house make the Palace still
His country mansion – Brixton Mill!

Quite a few people applied to the Tothill-fields authorities to be allowed to see the Boy as a curiosity. One of them was Charles Dickens, who wrote to Mr Francis Smedley, the High Sheriff of Westminster, on 1 April, that he very much wanted to come and see the 'Palace Victim', as he called the Boy Jones. Although Dickens was 'free' of most other London prisons, he had never previously been admitted to Tothill-fields Bridewell, but he thought his old acquaintance Smedley might put in a good word for him. Dickens greatly doubted the popular belief in the Boy's sharpness of intellect, perhaps having Barnaby Rudge in mind. The High Sheriff was clearly inclined to be helpful, since, on 17 April, Dickens wrote back to him announcing his intention to 'avail myself of your good offices in the matter of the "Boy Jones" as the Sunday newspapers denominate him in vary fat capitals'.[3] Unfortunately, Dickens left no record of his meeting with the Boy Jones, although the Boy crops up from time to time in Dickens's published writings. In one of his *Miscellaneous Papers*, 'Threatening Letter to Thomas Hood from an Ancient Gentleman', he waggishly notes that, if a father wants to train his not-particularly-gifted son to go to Court, there were three courses open to him: he must endeavour by artificial means to make him a dwarf, a wild man, or a Boy Jones. In a later article on the omniscient 'The Best Authority', Dickens writes that 'in respect of getting into the Queen's Palace, the Boy Jones was a fool to him'.[4]

Having heard the court gossip about the Boy Jones, the dandy and diarist Thomas Raikes wrote in his diary,

> A little scamp of an apothecary's errand boy, named Jones, has the
> unaccountable mania of sneaking privately into Buckingham Palace, where he
> is found secreted at night under a sofa, or some other hiding-place. No one can
> divine his object, but twice he has been detected and conveyed to the Police
> office, and put into confinement for a time. The other day he was detected in
> a third attempt, with apparently as little Object. Lady Sandwich wrote that he
> must undoubtedly be a descendant of In-I-Go Jones, the architect.[5]

This amusing pun on the name of the celebrated seventeenth-century
architect and theatre designer Inigo Jones was widely repeated in the
newspapers, although some attributed it to the poet Samuel Rogers rather
than to lady-in-waiting Lady Sandwich.[6]

As the Boy Jones was working the treadmill at Tothill-fields, his father was
still in high demand among the London curiosity-seekers, who tipped him a
few shillings or bought him drinks to have him talk about his notorious son.
On 26 May, Henry Jones was trudging home from his tailor's shop when some
gentlemen recognised him and invited him to a public house, where he was given
free access to the bar to make him more talkative about the Boy and his exploits.
At about two in the morning, Police Constable Wardlow, 87B, encountered
Henry Jones in Tothill-street. The old man was very drunk indeed, singing and
shouting at the top of his voice. When the police constable urged him to go
home, old Jones became combative, declaring that his intention was to 'go and
have a month with his dear boy'. He was taken into custody and charged with
being drunk and disorderly in the street.[7]

The morning after, a very worse-for-wear Henry Jones was placed at the bar
of Queen-square police court, where his son had stood back in 1838. On being
asked what excuse he might have for his extraordinary conduct, old Jones meekly
replied that some gentlemen had plied him with liquor until he must have become
quite drunk. When the magistrate Mr Gregorie asked what had happened to his
notorious son, Henry Jones replied that the Boy was still in prison. He had heard
that, when Edward was liberated, the government intended to do something for
him, perhaps send him to sea. Old Jones was fined two shillings and sixpence.

On 21 May, a man named William John Donovan was standing in front of
the House of Lords with a large placard:

Viscount Melbourne and the Boy Jones
From Jones's *Peep into the Palace*

	Dinners
Viscount Melbourne	867
E. Jones	4
	——
Majority for Lord Melbourne	863

Exactly what he wanted to accomplish by this bizarre demonstration is unclear, but he might have been a political radical, objecting to Lord Melbourne's great influence at court: one palace intruder was eating 867 dinners, the other only four. The police soon arrived and dragged Donovan away; he was charged with obstructing the pavement for the peers wanting to enter the House of Lords and fined five shillings.[8] The reference to 'Jones's *Peep into the Palace*' is curious, since there was really a radical pamphlet titled *A Peep in the Palace, or a Voice from the House of Correction*, by 'E. Jones, Visiter-Extraordinary to her Majesty'. Since it was probably suppressed, no copy exists in any library today, although one has survived in private hands.[9]

To say that this facetious short pamphlet makes a lot of sense would be an exaggeration, however. It was probably hastily written by some radical scribbler, who did his best to edify his readers about the Poor Law, under which the notorious Mother Brownrigg would have become the ideal workhouse matron. 'Men shall not have bread,' the corrupt government told the honest Britons, and it was up to spirited lads like the Boy Jones to show them the error of their ways. As a result, the Boy had gone from Palace to Prison, from rich crimson royal sofa to straw mattress; the horrid tread-wheel was propelled by feet that had proudly trod the regal carpets of England's Queen. A curious claim, which may actually be true, is that the Boy had turned down an offer of £20 from Madame Tussaud to model him in wax and exhibit him with the murderers Corder and Greenacre. There had been newspaper rumours that the royal flea catchers had been so busy after the Boy's visits that they had demanded a raise in salary, but the Boy asserted that he had carried no *live-stock* with him into the palace. Now, when he was in prison, the Queen could continue singing her lullaby to that 'noisy little squaller', the Princess Royal:

Rest, rest, royal Princess
Thy guards a watch keep
In the palace again
Young Jones can ne'er creep!

After the Boy Jones had been released from his second stint in prison, an enterprising journalist decided to write a book about him. It would be funny, he thought, to find out a little more about the Queen's stalker and to write a satirical account of his three visits to Buckingham Palace. After all, had the Boy not wanted to write a book about his adventures at the palace himself; perhaps all he required was a ghost-writer? A good title might be *A Night under the Queen's Bed*; surely, *that* would be the kind of book all Londoners would want to read!

The journalist went to Bell-yard, where he met Henry Jones, an elderly, grey-haired man, broken down by misfortune and infirmities. In 1822, he had married his sixteen-year-old employee, the needlewoman Mary Shores. By 1841, when Henry was sixty years old, they had seven children alive. Edward, the eldest, was the favourite of his doting mother, who had 'almost lost her reason' when he was arrested for the third time. He had been born on 7 April 1824, in Crown-court, Charlotte-street, Westminster, where the family had been residing at the time. All the children except the youngest boy, who was only two years old, had suffered badly from smallpox, as indicated by their pitted faces. The eldest daughter, fifteen-year-old Elizabeth, had gone blind from the disease but was still able to work as a needlewoman. Edward's younger sister Mary was already a servant girl, and although the ten-year-old twins George and John were still living at home, their schooling would soon have to be interrupted for them to earn their keep. Poor Henry Jones was still feeling the effects of the loan of upwards of £5 back in December 1838 to pay Mr Prendergast's fee; he had difficulties repaying his creditors and also delivering the monthly rent to the stony-hearted Mr James. The journalist could see that old Jones was not exaggerating in this respect, since the family were desperately poor. They were all living in one room, sleeping on miserable rags for want of proper beds. The ugly, stunted children were looking half starved.

Henry Jones explained that although Edward had left school before he was twelve years old, and although he had always been employed doing menial work, he could read and write quite well. For want of money to buy proper books, he instead purchased large bundles of scrap paper for a penny or two. Having to digest first some page of parliamentary reports, then a chapter from *British Birds*, and then another one from some overblown Gothic novel would hardly have satisfied most readers, but the Boy did not seem to mind as he sat by the fire poring over his grubby treasures. Edward had always had ideas above his station, Henry Jones explained. His manners were morose, gloomy and secretive. He had no confidants among his younger siblings, and treated them with disdain. Since he had always been lazy and reluctant to work, even the most liberal-minded employers, like the long-suffering Mr Griffiths, eventually had enough of him. He was fond of building cardboard houses and castles and nourished ideas of becoming an architect. Buckingham Palace and its inhabitants, particularly the Queen herself, were his prime interest in life. He still spoke about writing a book about life at the palace, sometimes making notes on scrap paper for this purpose.

When the journalist was eventually introduced to Edward himself, he shared the disappointment of many others who had met the celebrity of the day face to face. The Boy was short, pale and badly marked with smallpox. He was clearly fed up with visitors: 'On no occasion does he display any animation to dispel the gloom which naturally hangs upon his dull and lowering brow.' He refused to say how many times he had been in the palace, did not divulge how he had entered, and had nothing to tell about the many things he must have observed. He sat about at home all day, since he 'could not show his face near York-street, Westminster, without a crowd of boys following him, calling out "That's the boy who heard the princess cry!"'

The journalist must have left Bell-yard feeling quite disappointed, since after the promising revelations from Henry Jones, he probably expected more from the Boy himself. But having nothing truthful to tell has never put a journalist off when there was a good story about: he decided to use his imagination to produce a short satirical work about the Boy and his observations in Buckingham Palace. Adopting for himself the name Paul Pry the Elder, he explained to his readers that he was the editor of the Boy Jones's much-anticipated book about life at Buckingham Palace, containing the most astonishing revelations. But first, a funny poem, presumed to have been written by the Boy while still in confinement and sent to his editor and friend:

> Dear Paul, although in limbo fast, as erst have been my betters,
> Nor mind nor limb (thanks to the Queen) is yet subdued by fetters:
> And as I to the Palace went, that I might live in story,
> I gave you the honour due, to register my glory, –
> (For I'm a *Pry*, if not a *Paul*, and neither Whig or Tory).

> To register my glory, and the curious facts relate,
> For which I've Pry'd in bed chambers, and chambers, too, of state.
> From Kitchen Maids to Ministers, I've lots to tell of all;
> For when I saw them not, mine ear could well each voice recall
> From the lordly Melbourne's grunting tone, to the tiny baby's squall.

> For squall it does, and lustily, despite the nurses by
> However strange it may appear that *Princesses* should cry;
> They have their *tears*, like other folks, though prouder be their lot
> And *pain* is felt 'neath lofty domes, as well as thatch of cot.
> But as the poet (Byron, for I know no other) said –
> 'I won't philosophise' because, like him, 'I *will* be read!'

'Paul Pry' went on to describe his visit to the Joneses. Although he could not condone the Boy's visits to Buckingham Palace, it had been wrong to imprison him, since his only purpose had been to gather material for his book. Twice, the poor Boy had been sentenced to spend three months in a horrible Bastille, where he had been 'three parts starved and worked beyond endurance'. At the secret third examination, the Ministers had asked the Boy if he had come to steal potatoes, to spy on the court ladies when they were in a state of undress, or perhaps to carry off the infant princess. Other noble lords suspected that he had been hired by the Americans to promote republicanism by making fun of royalty, or by the Chartists to kill the Queen and put the crown on the head of the Mr John Frost, leader of the Newport Rising.

The Boy Jones ate and drank well during his multiple visits to Buckingham Palace, helping himself to plates of nourishing food from the kitchen. Although he had had to keep hidden during the daytime, he saw and heard much of interest. If we are to trust Paul Pry, the courtiers were always on the prowl for female company and the maids of honour notoriously unchaste. Once, the Boy was hidden in the nursery, where he heard Prince Albert sing a lullaby to the Princess:

> Oh hush thee, my darling
> Thy mother's the Queen
> Of the mightiest kingdom
> That ever was seen:
> And the Bishop will one day
> *Your* brow, too, anoint
> That is, if no boy put
> Your nose out of joint.
> So hush thee, and squall not so loudly, my duck
> Here's plenty of pap, and a sausage to suck!

The Prince then sang some more bawdy songs together with Lord Melbourne and the Boy Jones's erstwhile captor, the Baroness Lehzen:

> Oh! once I lived in Germany
> But in England now I am,
> For Queen Victoria sent for me,
> To look after her pet *Lamb*!

Paul Pry's fantasies end with the Boy hiding under the Queen's bed, watching all that is going on. Prince Albert comes into her bedroom, but since Queen Victoria is in a huff because of his rowdy singing with the Baroness, she seizes the chamber-pot to chase him away. At breakfast, they are better friends, however; although the Boy, hiding behind a screen, finds it odd that the Queen chides the Prince about him being a very poor rider, who might well need some help from some sturdy English grooms!

In the end, Paul Pry thought *A Night under the Queen's Bed* a somewhat daring title for his masterpiece. Fearing that the book might be withdrawn, he changed it to *Royal Secrets; or A Pry in the Palace*.[10] This thirty-two-page book was published in July 1841 and advertised in the *Odd Fellow* newspaper. Disappointingly, it was not illustrated with the portrait of the

Boy Jones, but instead with an engraving of the Queen, Prince and Princess. Paul Pry threatened that the Boy might well be writing a second volume of royal secrets, to be published later in the year, as he expressed it in laborious verse, alleged to come from the imprisoned Boy:

> But soft – confound the turnkey! He informs me it is time
> To be locked up till morning, so tonight farewell to rhyme.
> But in my next epistle, such a flare-up will be seen
> As will astonish all who read, including England's Queen.

> For read my book, she must and will; Her Majesty well knows
> I'm bothered for a rhyme, dear Paul, and must my letter close;
> But this shall not occur again, my next shall be in prose.
> So (again I hear a growling, in the jailor's husky tones)
> No more at the present time from your faith-ful prying friend NED JONES!

But as the journalists and satirical writers were extolling the Boy Jones in prose and verse, Queen Victoria and her ministers were not amused. The Boy seemed to have some uncanny ability to enter the palace, and what guarantee was there that he would not develop into a royal assassin like Edward Oxford, brandishing a brace of pistols at the terrified Queen in her bedroom, or using the royal crib for target practice? Lord Melbourne's government seems to have made the decision that enough was enough: this time, they had to get rid of the Boy Jones for good, just like the author of *A Peep in the Palace* had predicted:

> Sleep, sleep, royal Princess
> Pray, pray cease thy cry;
> Under the royal sofa,
> Jones shall ne'er again lie!

> Nor sit on the throne
> Nor hide under our bed;
> If he comes here again,
> *We will cut off his head*!

5

The Mysterious Disappearance of the Boy Jones

Boy Jones, in scoring high has got a fall;
Better he had not tried to climb at all;
Yet *some* severer doom have found than his'n
When from a *Palace* they've been sent to *prison*!

From the *Satirist*, 21 March 1841.

After he had been released from prison for the second time on 14 June 1841, the existence of the Boy Jones was as miserable as ever. According to the instructions from the Home Office, he had been worked very hard on the treadmill and fed an extremely low diet; as a result, he had been almost reduced to a skeleton. He could not find employment, people mocked and jeered him, and he thought strange men were following him about in the streets. The latter were no figments of his imagination, but police agents employed to monitor the activities of the palace intruder. They could report that, although the Boy sometimes went for a stroll to Constitution Hill, he never attempted to climb the wall there.

A steady stream of curiosity-seekers still greased Henry Jones's palm at the Bell-yard hovel, wanting to see the Boy, but Edward had tired of the role of a sideshow freak and sat in sulky silence instead of amusing his guests with some spicy anecdotes about the goings-on at Buckingham Palace. A manager of one of the minor theatres called to offer him £4 per week to appear on stage for two weeks, with a 'benefit' at the end of this period. It is not stated in what way he was supposed to entertain the audience. Complaining that two weeks was too short a period for him to exhibit himself, the Boy turned the offer down.[1]

Another visitor was an aspiring playwright, who offered £50 for Edward to appear in his play *The Sweep in the Palace* for three months. This time, Henry Jones willingly agreed, but the Boy said, 'If my father and mother force me on the stage I will insult the audience!' To try to tempt Edward into a stage career, the playwright offered the dirty, stunted fellow a watch and a suit of clothes, but the Boy haughtily said, 'The stage is not sufficiently respectable for me – I think I can do better!' Mystified, the playwright asked what he meant. With an almost regal gesture to a shabby cardboard house he had built, the Boy responded, 'To become an architect!' This almost surreal conversation seems to have convinced the playwright that Edward was a very odd boy indeed, and his usefulness as an actor extremely limited.[2]

The only solace for the Boy and his family was that the aforementioned publican Mr William James, the Jones's landlord, seemed to have undergone some strange personality change. No longer did he pester them for the rent or annoy them with his habitual mean-spiritedness, but instead he assured Henry Jones that he was a firm friend of the family. He freely offered to help old Jones's blind daughter Elizabeth into an asylum, and to make sure the Boy received paid employment. Mr James had several friends living near Regent's Park, he claimed, and if he were allowed to take the Boy with him for a short country excursion, he would do his best to obtain him a situation with one of them. Henry Jones readily agreed, but it turned out that none of Mr James's wealthy friends needed a domestic servant. Instead, the publican brought with him a friend, Mr James Christopher Evans, who introduced himself as a shipping agent, with good contacts in London's maritime world. Surely, for someone like him, it would not be difficult to get the Boy paid employment as a seaman.

Mr James explained that he and his friend knew a certain Captain Taylor, of the ship *Diamond*, who was looking for an apprentice seaman. Captain Taylor was a good and kindly man and would take on Edward as an apprentice for three years. If he proved satisfactory, he would be paid not less than £30 per annum. Each time the ship was in London, he would be allowed to come home to his family. The *Diamond* would set sail from London Docks in just a few days' time, for Port William in New Zealand, so the Boy and his father had to make up their minds quickly if they wanted to take advantage of this great offer.

But, as we know, Henry Jones was not one for decisive action. For several days, he kept helplessly vacillating about what was the best action to take. Edward preferred a job on land, but could a boy with his kind of notoriety ever get one? And was this offer, made to a young lad with no maritime experience whatsoever, not just a little too good to be true? But a few days later, the tempter Mr James returned. After a good deal of discussion, he persuaded Henry Jones and Edward to accompany him to Blackwall, where Captain Taylor was staying, to have an interview with this benevolent mariner.

But when they came to Blackwall, it turned out that the *Diamond* had already sailed for Gravesend. Instead, the mysterious Mr Evans was waiting for the Joneses in a comfortable Blackwall tavern. If they wanted to make use of his offer, he tempted them, he and Mr James would have to bring Edward with them to Gravesend without delay. But where would the Boy get money for his outfit as a sailor, penniless old Henry Jones dithered. With a grand gesture, Mr Evans brought up a purse of gold guineas and promised that if Captain Taylor accepted Edward and agreed to take him with him on the voyage, he himself would give a grant of five sovereigns to pay for his equipment.

Poor Henry Jones must have felt quite dizzy and confused. What were these two men really intending, and could they be relied upon? But the sight of the five gold coins enticed him, deprived him of whatever remnant of common sense he still possessed. He agreed to let them take Edward away to Gravesend, but only if he himself could also accompany the party. But reverting to his former nastiness, Mr James said that this might not be such a good idea, since Henry Jones was very shabbily dressed and not at all the person to give a favourable impression; if old Jones came along, the publican said, there would be a considerable risk that Captain Taylor would turn Edward down. The Boy would not be gone for very long, he continued, since as soon as the Captain had taken Edward on, he would be driven back to his parents the very same evening.

The thought of his son returning to Bell-yard in triumph, with his five gold guineas, was enough to persuade the weak-willed Henry Jones that all was well and that he could fully trust his two newfound friends and benefactors. Accordingly, Mr James and Mr Evans drove off with Edward, and Henry Jones waved merrily to them as the carriage passed him by. He called out to his son that he would see him later in the evening, but a voice from the carriage responded, 'You will see him when you see him!' It is not known whether this rather sinister response caused Henry Jones any misgivings as the slow-witted old man was pondering recent events during his long trudge back to Bell-yard.

Henry Jones and his family waited all night, but Edward did not return. The next morning, old Jones went up to the Bell to ask for Mr James, but he was curtly told that the publican was not expected to be home for several days. Thinking that this sounded sinister, Henry Jones belatedly became seriously worried about his son. In breathless haste, he proceeded to a shipping office. This pathetic scene would not have been out of place in a Dickens novel: the careworn old man entering the office despondently wringing his gnarled hands, almost forgetting to politely doff his cap to the shipping clerk before he asked some questions about the *Diamond*. Did he inwardly dread each answer, fearing or even guessing the answers after his sluggish brain had finally succeeded in making the deductions it should have made the day before? Was he shown fear in a handful of dust, slowly and inexorably, in the clerk's simple answers? Henry Jones was told that this ship had left Gravesend for Cork. When the old man asked what was the cargo, and when the *Diamond* could be expected to return to London, the shipping clerk laughed. Did he not know that the *Diamond* was an *emigrant ship*?

We can only guess what further pathetic scenes took place in the Bell-yard hovel when the heartbroken old man announced to his wife and children that Edward probably had been shanghaied on board an emigrant ship, on its way to Port Philip in New Zealand. Henry Jones tried to obtain information from the Home Office and at the Bow Street magistrates court, but was met with stony silence. The perfidious Mr James was still not at home, and timid old Henry Jones was ill-equipped to fight alone against a hostile world. Let down by the government, magistrates and police, he spoke to the *Times* journalist who had interviewed him previously. Henry Jones told him that his son had complained very much about the way he had been treated at Tothill-fields and attributed it entirely to the orders of the government. Now he had been abducted by Mr James, and the mysterious Mr Evans, and was probably on his way to New Zealand.

On 7 July, the *Times* journalist published his article, after having made some further researches. His findings were unlikely to have given much cheer to the beleaguered Jones family, however. The article announced that the notorious Boy Jones, who had caused so much mischief, had now been 'taken quietly in hand by the proper authorities'.[3] In prison, Jones had been quiet and orderly, the journalist claimed, and never given the governor any cause for complaint. After being released, he had been secretly watched by the police. They could report that although he had frequently been seen on Constitution Hill, and even in the vicinity of Buckingham Palace, there was nothing in his manner or behaviour different from all the other people frequenting these parks in hopes of obtaining a sight of royalty. Still, he was considered a dangerous character, likely to be meditating another entrance into the palace. 'The proper authorities' had placed him on board the *Diamond* emigration ship, the journalist wrote. There were differing opinions how exactly this had been accomplished. The Boy's father believed that two mysterious men had taken him to Gravesend and that he had been apprenticed as a seaman for three years. Another story told that an officer of the Thames Police had been put in charge of disposing of the Boy Jones and that this individual had left London by railway, bringing the Boy with him. There had been strict orders 'to those in whose charge he was not to lose sight of him until he was on board the *Diamond* in the harbour of Cork'. He would be apprenticed as a seaman for five years, after which period he would be found employment in Australia or New Zealand.

Poor Henry Jones's head must have been swimming when he read this sinister article. Had his son been shanghaied not just once, but twice? Was he in Gravesend, in Cork, or on the ocean wave on his way to New Zealand? And would he be kept away from his family, like some miserable galley slave, for an untold number of years? Some answers were provided by a mysterious letter that arrived at the Jones household a few days later, bearing the postmark of Cork:

Cork, July 7, 1841.

Dear Father – I am glad to inform you Mr. James, his friend (a police officer), and myself, since leaving Westminster, are well. I have experienced the utmost friendship from Mr. James. In earnest, I wish the same never to be forgot. Having a good recommendation, I am happy and in excellent spirits.

Finally, I hope all of you are well. Please to inform Mrs. James that Mr. James intends to take a tour through Ireland, and will not, therefore, return for ten days. I am on my road through Bristol.

Edward Jones

P.P. My kind love to all my brothers and sisters, and I hope evermore they will become good children.[4]

This letter, obviously intended to answer the queries in the *Times* article and reassure the Jones family that Edward was still alive and well, had exactly the opposite effect. What on earth was the Boy doing in Cork? Had he been taken there in the *Diamond* and been left behind, or had Mr James and Mr Evans just pretended to go to Gravesend and instead transported the Boy to Ireland by some other means? Even to simple-minded people like the Joneses, it was clear that this bizarre letter with its stilted phrases had been dictated to Edward by some person wanting to deceive his family in London. After the word 'Bristol' had been written, it had been heavily crossed out by some person, but it was still legible.

We now have to leave sad old Henry Jones and his family behind to rejoin the two kidnappers, Mr James and Mr Evans. These villains must have been in good cheer after successfully enticing Edward Jones away from his father in Blackwall and driving him to Gravesend. They kept playing their roles: Mr James was the benevolent neighbour and Mr Evans the equally kind-hearted shipping agent, who was willing to give away five guineas to help his young friend establish his maritime career. Soon, they would meet that hearty old salt Captain Taylor, and the Boy Jones would become a jolly Jack Tar on his way to new adventures on the ocean wave!

But things did not go as planned, not by any means. It would appear that when the Home Office had employed the publican William James as a secret agent, with a mission to make sure that the Boy Jones left London permanently, he had been partnered with James Christopher Evans, junior, an Inspector of the Thames Police. It was thought that the cunning, mean-spirited publican would be able to lure the Boy away from his family and that the experienced Thames police officer would find an unscrupulous skipper to take him to some distant colony, far from Buckingham Palace and its inhabitants. It had probably been debated whether to make the Boy emigrate permanently or to enrol him as an apprentice seaman for some considerable period of time. Since the *Diamond* offered the opportunity for either of these alternatives, the two secret agents approached Captain Taylor, offering him a tidy sum of money to take a young emigrant boy on board at Blackwall. As we know, this plan failed due to the dithering of Henry Jones, but the two rogues managed to catch up with the *Diamond* at Gravesend.

But when the two secret agents were at the brink of completing the mission and getting rid of the Boy Jones, things went disastrously wrong. One of Captain Taylor's officers had had the Boy Jones pointed out to him in London, and when the sinister-looking urchin was led on board by his two abductors, this officer immediately identified him as London's great criminal celebrity. The choleric Captain Taylor went berserk. So *this* was the young boy they had wanted to 'export' abroad! The scoundrel who had been found lurking near the Queen's bedroom and about whom so much had been written in the London newspapers! Even if they paid him £500, or any other sum, he refused to allow such a miscreant on board his ship![5]

When Inspector Evans pointed out that they had made a deal that the captain would accept the Boy, the barking of the royalist old sea dog became even more furious. It was the inspector who had been deceiving, not he, since it had not been made clear to him that it was the infamous Boy Jones they were talking about! Were they thinking they could sell Captain Taylor, of the *Diamond*, a pig in the poke, and foist upon him the most infernal scoundrel who ever lived, the miserable vagabond who had been caught spying in the Queen's dressing room ... Fearing that the Captain's bite would be as bad as his bark, the two secret agents hastily made their way to dry land, with the Boy Jones in tow. After a brief council of war, Mr James and Inspector Evans decided to make their way back to London, to consult the resident spymaster at the Home Office. History does not relate how they fared in this confrontation, except that their orders were to proceed to Cork using the greatest possible expedition, catch up with the *Diamond*, and persuade Captain Taylor to take the Boy Jones on board.

Although they may well have had misgivings about the prospect of persuading the fierce Captain Taylor to accept the Boy, the two secret agents obediently set out for Cork. It can only be guessed exactly what means they used to discipline the Boy Jones during this lengthy journey. According to the *Times* journalist quoted earlier, their orders had been not to lose sight of him until he was on board the *Diamond*. They made it all the way to Cork, where they successfully intercepted the *Diamond*, only to find that Captain Taylor's short temper had not improved in the slightest. All they got for their trouble was another volley of abuse from the forthright old sea dog. Returning to dry land to lick their wounds, the two secret agents considered their options. The Home Office had not provided them with a 'Plan B' if the volatile Captain Taylor turned them down again, and they suspected that if they returned to London with the Boy Jones in tow, they would be harshly criticised for this bungled attempt to dispose of the Queen's stalker.

But either the mean-spirited publican or the unconventional police inspector thought of a cunning plan. Cork was full of Irish emigrants, many of whom were planning to travel on the *Diamond*. At a tavern, the two secret agents made friends with a young Irish lad, whom they bribed with part of the money promised to Captain Taylor to *play the part* of the Boy Jones on board the *Diamond*. Once at sea, he would tell some of the other passengers that he was the palace intruder, about whom so much had been written in the newspapers. And when the ship reached Port William, he would make sure that it was made known that the celebrated Boy Jones had arrived. Even if the Home Office had ordered some colonial official in Port William to make sure the Boy Jones arrived on shore, this individual would not know what the Boy looked like and would thus be fooled by the impostor.

This disreputable plan seems to have worked quite well. The young Irish lad, whose name we do not know, played his role with enthusiasm. Tom Clancy, one of the 330 emigrants on board the *Diamond*, was amazed at the yarns he told about visiting the Queen, although some of the other emigrants were not taken in by his stories.[6] This charade did not end when the *Diamond* arrived at Melbourne. A few days later, the *Port Philip Patriot* wrote that 'the boy Jones, whose repeated intrusions into Buckingham Palace is well known, arrived as an immigrant on the *Diamond*'.

But although the Irish lad did his best, the Australian journalists found him out. Three weeks later, the same newspaper wrote,

> The boy Jones is not it seems on board the *Diamond* after all. He was taken to Cork to be put on board, but Captain Taylor refused to have anything to do with him. The Government had contrived to have him smuggled out of the country but whether he has gone, even his father is ignorant. There is a boy on board the *Diamond* who represents himself to be the boy in question.[7]

As the Irish impostor was amusing his fellow emigrants on board the *Diamond* with his tall tales of serial palace intrusion, things were not going very well for those two disreputable secret agents, William James and James Christopher Evans. They seem to have decided that once they had planted the impostor on board the *Diamond*, the next step was to find another ship, with another unscrupulous captain, willing to take the Boy Jones away to some faraway country. For this purpose, they went to Bristol, and then to Plymouth, but without any success. One would have imagined that there would have been no shortage of more or less crooked skippers in the Bristol and Plymouth docks, ready to accept a bribe to make the Boy 'disappear' abroad, but this does not appear to have been the case. Perhaps the sight of the dirty, stunted Boy, with his two sinister attendants, arose suspicion even among the roughest mariners of these parts. Mr James and Inspector Evans must have been becoming increasingly desperate. Would they be doomed to travel for evermore, seeking some means to dispose of England's state prisoner, the albatross tied around their necks?

Had this book been a novel, the next chapter would probably have involved a desolate country lane, a well-aimed blow with a shovel, and a shallow grave by the roadside. The publican William James seems to have been one of nature's 'bad guys', who delighted in deceiving honest but dim-witted people and kicking those who were already down. But although Mr James and Inspector Evans were scoundrels of the blackest hue, as judged from their villainous deceit against the Joneses, there is no evidence to suggest that either of them ever contemplated murdering the Boy.[8] After all, they both had positions and families in London. Henry Jones had a fairly good idea who had taken the Boy and also some degree of contact with the newspaper press.

No, the publican and the inspector had orders to make sure the Boy Jones was shanghaied on board a ship, and shanghaied he must be. After another council of war, they set off for Liverpool, where Inspector Evans expected the needy mariners to be more appreciative of his bribes. And here the two scoundrels finally struck lucky. In Liverpool Docks, they met a Captain Ramsay, of the ship *Tiber*, destined for Bahia, Brazil. After his palm had been greased by Inspector Evans, he willingly agreed to take the Boy on board, although the new recruit had to be approved also by the ship's agent. Fearful that the Gravesend debacle would be repeated, and that the agent or some other person would recognise the Boy as the palace intruder, the two secret agents bought a large wig and put it on Edward's head as a disguise. When the agent asked why the Boy wore the wig, they said he had suffered badly from the ringworm. This disreputable stratagem had the desired effect: the Boy Jones was accepted as a ship's boy on board the *Tiber*, and Mr James and Inspector Evans were finally free of their bothersome charge.

It is not known if the two secret agents stood on the quayside waving goodbye to the Boy Jones as the *Tiber* left Liverpool Docks, but it is a fact that yet another extraordinary letter, with a Liverpool postmark, arrived at the Jones household in Bell-yard. This time, it was dated Liverpool, 15 July 1841, and contained the following words:

Dear Father, – In my progress I am glad to inform you Mr James has entertained me with kindness. Our earnest views is ended. A pleasant voyage to Brazil with me, with a good captain. You will add a calm to my mind in believing your son hopes you are all well; finally I am in health.

My writings or otherwise keep them with carefulness.

Believe me, &c.

P.S. England is a most magnificent country. Her inhabitants are a most gracious people. I declare the same inasmuch as I have experienced a kind regard from several persons. At the present time I am greatly extolled by Mr James; his earnest views are promoting the welfare of deserving individuals, pursuant to establishing them in orderly courses. I trust I may declare that my kind friend in the present case is a neighbour who has acted on a greater interest than generally.[9]

This second letter, as sinister as the first, aroused novel consternation among the Joneses. Was poor Edward really going to Brazil? And had he been pressed on board ship or gone voluntarily? Incapable of solving the mystery on his own, Henry Jones again appealed to the *Times* journalist who had proved so knowledgeable in the past; all this individual could recommend was to wait for the return of Mr James and his friend the shipping agent.

It would take until early August for Mr James to return to Bell-yard, after an absence of more than a month. Had Henry Jones been a forceful character, he would have waited for the deceiving publican with a horsewhip or a blunt instrument at hand, but as we know, the old tailor was meek, timid and respectful towards his betters. When he begged Mr James for information about his son, he was brusquely told that Edward was on his way to Brazil in a ship of 270 tons burden and that his first voyage would occupy nine months. Mr James refused to give the name of the ship, or of the captain, and maintained an ominous silence when asked what plans had been made for the Boy when he returned after nine months. With his usual nastiness, Mr James bragged about his cunning strategy to put a wig on the Boy's head to disguise him; he probably laughed heartily when the simple-minded Henry Jones objected that his son had never been afflicted with the ringworm.

Henry Jones was 'exceedingly anxious to ascertain whether the boy has gone abroad known as the boy discovered in Buckingham Palace', since if this were the case, he would surely be 'subject to great annoyance' like he had been in London before he was abducted. Mr James remained silent on this point; nor would he say whether Edward had sailed under his own name or whether another name had been assumed. After impressing on his tenant 'that nothing should be said on the subject if any inquiries were made of the family', the mean-spirited publican returned to ply his long-neglected trade.

But, for once, Henry Jones made a valiant attempt to stand up to his landlord and tormentor. He went to the *Times* journalist and again poured out his long tale of woe. The newspaper man could sense a good story, full of what we today would call human interest: 'The father states that for some time his wife was inconsolable, and it was with difficulty he could assume sufficient courage to enable him to follow his humble occupation.' They had both been bordering on distraction due to the state of uncertainty about their child. From 'the mystery, secrecy, and extraordinary circumstances attending this truly singular case', the journalist suspected that some very high and powerful people had been conspiring against the hapless Boy Jones. They had employed at least three people to make sure the Boy Jones disappeared, he speculated: Mr James, the mysterious ship's agent Evans, and the unnamed police inspector. Who had been paying for their month of perpetual travelling with the Boy: from London to Gravesend, back to London, then to Cork, Bristol, Plymouth and Liverpool? Deservedly, Mr James also received his fair share of newspaper criticism. Since the *Times* article had referred to him as 'a gentleman', another paper delivered a hurtful put-down as it sneered that he was only the kind of *gentleman* that keeps a public house.

There was a brief newspaper debate about the legality of abducting a young boy and forcibly sending him abroad as a sailor before the mast. Quoting a recent case where a magistrate had declared that trespassing into a house was no criminal offence unless it was with the intent to steal something, the *Examiner* questioned 'if this be sound law, for what was the boy Jones imprisoned? Mr Clive's doctrine will be a great comfort and encouragement to all persons of a curious turn of mind, who will like to see what is going on in houses without invitations.'[10] The *John Bull* newspaper was even more scathing. They wondered why 'Jones, poor child, really is considered by the Ministers a dangerous character'. Surely, the fact that 'the proper authorities' could just make a young boy 'disappear' to sea must be a sign that 'the worst days of the Inquisition and the Bastille are come again'? And was it not an enormity that the laws were outraged, Constitution violated and public justice perverted, for the mere purpose of preventing a small boy from entering the Queen's palace?[11] Another newspaper had heard that when the Boy Jones had been errand-boy to the surgeon Mr Campbell, of the Broadway, Westminster, he had once been overheard to express his determination to enter Buckingham Palace again. The gentleman who heard him wrote to the Marquess of Normanby, who did nothing at all about it. The Boy ought to have been flogged for his intrusion in December 1840, the police for the one in March 1841, and that careless minister, the Marquess of Normanby, for both. But no, 'this formidable opponent of the Whig Ministers must be taken by his pretended friend, a policeman, and pressed on board some vessel going to the same place to which Whig Ministers are bound – the devil knows where. Poor boy! Poor Whigs! We pity one, but we despise the other!'[12]

But as the Tory newspapers were trying to raise an opinion about the abduction of the Boy Jones, week after week went by with no news about the shanghaied Boy. Following his defeat in the 1841 election, Lord Melbourne resigned on 30 August and Sir Robert Peel became the new Prime Minister. His policy with regard to serial palace intruders did not differ from that of his predecessor, however. The reason the Tory newspapers had taken up the cudgel for the Boy Jones in the first place had of course been that they wanted to annoy the Melbourne government; after Peel had been sworn into office, their enthusiasm for espousing the case of the palace intruder quickly waned.

Still there was no news about the poor Edward. As a last resort, the distraught Henry Jones began visiting the police offices, hoping that some person would have pity on him. In November, he waited on the magistrate at the Thames police court, when he suddenly recognised a person he knew very well: it was the mysterious Mr Evans, the 'shipping agent' who had helped to abduct the Boy back in July. But he was wearing the uniform of a Thames police inspector! When old Jones challenged him and 'expressed his surprise that a police officer should represent himself as the agent of a ship', Evans quickly improvised that he had in fact been moonlighting as the agent of a ship at the time, and all that had been done for the Boy had been for his benefit. Henry Jones said that he, the boy's father, ought to have been consulted about the matter, or at least informed about the destination of the ship. Evans replied that the Boy's 'interests would have been materially affected if his destination had become known' and spoke highly of his young charge's intelligence and good conduct. Recent events had taught old Jones to recognise a liar and hypocrite, however, and he demanded to see the magistrate, fearing that his son would be sent away to sea again, but the agitated old man was informed that this would be pointless since the magistrate had no jurisdiction in the matter.[13]

6

Shanghaied Again!

Oakum to me, ye sailors bold,
Wot plows upon the sea;
For you I mean for to unfold
My mournful histo-ree.
So pay attention to my song,
And quick-el-ly shall appear,
How innocently, all along,
I wos in-weigle-ed here.

One night, returnin' home to bed,
I walk'd through Pim-li-co,
And, twigging of the Palass, sed,
'I'm *Jones* and *In-i-go.*'
But before I could get out, my boys
Polliseman 20 A,
He caught me by the courderoys,
And lugged me right a-way.

My cuss upon Lord Melbun, and
On Johnny Russ-all-so,
They forc'd me from my native land
Across the waves to go-o-oh.
But all their spiteful arts is vain,
My spirits down to keep;
I hopes I'll soon get back again,
To take another peep.

From *The Boy Jones's Log, picked up at Sea* in *Punch*, 7 August 1841, p. 46.
Oakum was naval talk for 'Oh come', the article facetiously alleged.

On 10 December 1841, Henry Jones received a soiled letter with a Liverpool postmark. To his great joy, it turned out to be from Edward. He had been forced to sail to Bahia and back on board the *Tiber*, not returning to Liverpool until 30 November. He was heartily tired of seafaring life, for which he had never had any liking, and had been subjected to much ill-usage on board. The brutal Captain Ramsay and his boatswains had worked poor Edward very hard, and whipped him mercilessly for any shortcoming or misdemeanour. Now, Edward was left stranded in Liverpool, after having been paid just two shillings and sixpence for four months of hard work. He was fearful that he would again be abducted and forced to sail abroad, a concern that was fully shared by his father, whose feeble intellect had by this time been able to digest the full extent of Mr James's perfidy. The letter ended with a request for travel money so that the Boy could return to his family in London.[1]

Henry Jones was nearly as penniless as his son, however, and they lacked the means for even the cheapest kind of transportation. The stolid, uncomplaining old man once more began trudging round the neighbourhood, borrowing pennies and farthings to buy his errant son a ticket back to London. But due to either homesickness, impatience, or perhaps also lack of faith in his elderly parent's ability to raise money, Edward bought a loaf of bread for his final pennies and began his long tramp toward the Metropolis. When he had eaten his bread, the starving boy had to subsist, for several days, on rock-hard turnips that he picked in the fields. He slept in barns and outhouses, wrapped in rags to avoid freezing to death. On 18 December, after a journey of 210 miles, the newspapers could report that Boy Jones had arrived home very footsore and exhausted.[2]

There was immediate interest from the Boy's old journalist friends. The bogus story that he had been sent to New Zealand on board the *Diamond* could now be definitely discounted, in favour of the version that he had been forced to go to sea by that villainous pair, Mr James and Inspector Evans. Among the newspapers, there were three rival factions. Firstly, several papers, the conservative *Times* and *John Bull* prominent among them, remained actively pro-Jones. When *The Times* interviewed poor Henry Jones while Edward was still in Liverpool, the old tailor said he had been unable to follow his usual occupation during the last week, due to his distress of mind. He intended to write to the port authorities in Liverpool, requesting them not to allow his son to 'be trepanned into another journey'.[3] There was good reason to fear that such an attempt might be made by government agents, the journalist agreed. Was this merry old England, where common people were treated fairly by their superiors, a France with its Bastille and its galley-slaves, or a Russia ruled by a dismal tyrant who could make his unwanted subjects 'disappear' forever into some secret prison?

The anti-Jones *Age* newspaper was much more critical about what it called 'the renewal of the humbug about this little troublesome, inquisitive, dirty *snob*'. Lord Normanby had done his best to rid the Londoners of Master Jones, but now the palace intruder had returned like a bad penny, and 'the humanity-mongers of the great metropolis' were immediately on his side.

Moving on to some puns, the journalist wrote,

> Master Jones did not like the sea – he was *sick* of it.
> So are most people on their first journey – *O! sic omnes*.
> He begged to be put ashore and wept bitterly when refused –
> Not contented with annoying the crew by being *sick*,
> He added to the annoyance by his mu-*sic*!

Since he was so very fond of palaces and seeing what was going on at Court, the Boy Jones should be employed as a servant at some *gin-palace* in some *court* or other, since many curiosity-seeking people 'would be induced to risk their health by absorbing Hodges' best to get a sight of the boy who got a sight of Royalty while under the Royal sofa.'[4]

The comic papers went on with their usual fun. The Boy's old friend the *Satirist* invented an amusing letter from Edward to his father:

> The warmint! That ever I should be trapped into a seafaring life! I was sea-sick at starting, and I never got over it. ... What say you, father, to another Palace rig? I have not forgot the secret way over the wall, and through the low garden window. ... I shall roam about o'nights, and rummage the Queen's apartments, and rumfusticate the Maids of Honour whenever I meets 'em. I mean to frighten the nurses into fits; that's one of the first things I means to do; and arter that I means to pay my respects to her blessed Majesty herself.[5]

After thrice sneaking into Buckingham Palace, twice going to prison, and suffering the additional indignity of being kidnapped, shanghaied, and forced to work his way from Liverpool to Bahia and back before the mast, the life of Edward Jones seemed to return to a rare state of normality in early January 1842. His father had made an agreement with Mr W. Elgar, a respectable tobacconist of No. 17 Tothill-street, that Edward was to serve this gentleman as errand-boy for twelve months. Initially, the Boy made good progress in his new occupation. Pleased to be spared the cruelty and hard work on board ship, he declared that life in the tobacconist's shop suited him very well. He was paid regularly and the duties were relatively light. Both Mr Elgar and the various customers who frequented the shop and the cigar and coffee rooms above stairs were quite satisfied with the new servant.[6] It has to be suspected that Mr Elgar's offer to employ Edward had not entirely been motivated by human kindness, but also by the use of the notorious Boy Jones to attract curiosity-seeking customers to the cigar rooms, just like the *Age* journalist had suggested.

But the respectable tobacconist would not have long to enjoy the success of this stratagem. Edward told him that mysterious men were lounging about outside the cigar shop. One of them was dressed as midshipman, another as a sailor with what looked like a large false beard. More than once, the 'midshipman'

1. The young Queen Victoria, from vol. 2 of the *Gallery of Engravings*. (Author's collection)

2. Queen Victoria leaves Buckingham Palace for a visit to the City of London, from the *Mirror* of 1838. (Author's collection)

3. Another engraving of the young Queen Victoria, from a portrait by Dalton after F. Winterhalter. (Author's collection)

Top: 4. A contemporary engraving of Buckingham Palace. (Author's collection)

Right: 5. The young Queen Victoria, an engraving from a portrait by E. J. Parris. (Author's collection)

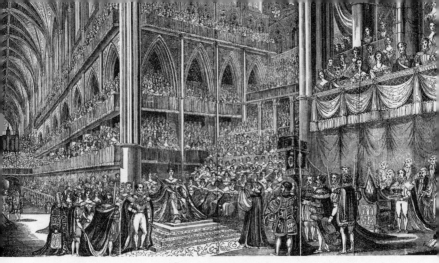

6. The coronation of Queen Victoria, from the *Mirror* of 1838. (Author's collection)

7. The parents of Queen Victoria, the Duke and Duchess of Kent, from vol. 2 of the *Gallery of Engravings* and the *Mirror* of 1838, respectively. (Author's collection)

A SHOWER OF GERMAN PAUPERS,
OR BAD WEATHER FOR JOHN BULL.

8. The young Prince Albert, an engraving from a portrait by Dalton after F. Winterhalter. (Author's collection)

Top: 9. A Shower of German Paupers, an anti-Albert cartoon in the Penny Satirist of 14 March 1840. (Author's collection)

10. Queen Victoria and Prince Albert, an engraving from a portrait on stone by Lover. (Author's collection)

11. Edward Oxford shoots at the Queen and Prince Albert, from a contemporary print. (Author's collection)

12. Lord Melbourne, an engraving from the portrait by Sir Edwin Landseer. (Author's collection)

13. The Duke of Wellington and Sir Robert Peel, an engraving from the portrait by Winterhalter. (Author's collection)

14. Edward Oxford, from an old print. (Author's collection)

15. Baroness Lehzen depicted by Queen Victoria herself; from Viscount Esher, *The Girlhood of Queen Victoria*, Vol. 2 (London, 1912). (Author's collection)

A STRANGER IN HER MAJESTY'S BEDROOM.
THE BOY JONES AGAIN!
"What will Mrs. Grundy say—Mrs. Lilley?"

On Wednesday, shortly after 12 o'clock, the inmates of Buckingham Palace were aroused by an alarm being given that a stranger had been discovered under the sofa in her Majesty's dressing-room. The domestics and officers of the household were immediately in motion, and it was soon ascertained that the alarm was not without foundation. The daring intruder was immediately secured, and safely handed over to the custody of the police.

The inquiry into this mysterious circumstance has created the most intense interest at Buckingham Palace and the west-end of the of the town, where the report spread with the rapidity of lightning. At first it was not generally believed, but when it was known that the prisoner was under examination at the Home Office public curiosity was at its height, and inquiries into the most minute particulars were made in every place where it was likely to obtain information respecting an event which might, under present circumstances, have been attended with most dangerous effects to the health of our beloved Queen.

Shortly after 12 o'clock one of her Majesty's pages, attended by other domestics of the royal household, went into her Majesty's dressing-room, which adjoins the bed-chamber in which the Queen's accouchement took place. Whilst there they imagined that they heard a noise. A strict search was commenced, and under the sofa on which her Majesty had been sitting only about two hours before they discovered a dirty, ill-looking fellow, who was immediately dragged from his hiding-place, and given into the custody of Inspector Stead, then on duty at the Palace. The prisoner immediately underwent a strict search, but no weapon of any dangerous nature was found on his person. He was afterwards conveyed to the station in Gardener's Lane, and handed over to Inspector Haining, of the A division of police, with instructions to keep him in safe custody until he received further orders from the Home Office. We understand that as soon as the prisoner was hand-d over to the police he was immediately recognised as the same person who effected such an extraordinary entrance into Buckingham Palace about two years since, for which offence he was tried at the Westminster Sessions and acquitted, the jury being of opinion that he was not right in his mind. It may here be stated that the name of the daring intruder into the abode of royalty is Edward Jones; he is 17 years of age. In person the prisoner is very short of his age, and has a most repulsive appearance; he was very meanly dressed, but affected an air of great consequence; he repeatedly requested the police to address him in a becoming manner, and to behave towards him as they ought to do to a gentleman who was anxious to make a noise in the world.

At 12 o'clock on Thursday the prisoner was brought in custody of the police to the Home Office, and shortly afterwards taken before the Council, when, we understand, he was interrogated as to his motives for such extraordinary conduct, and particularly as to the mode by which he obtained an entrance into the Palace. He (the prisoner) told their lordships that he was willing to point out to the police the way he effected an entrance, and to state all particulars. Their lordships, on this statement, directed the police immediately to convey Jones to Buckingham Palace, and obtain the information he promised to give, and adjourned the inquiry until half past two o'clock.

The prisoner was taken to the Palace, and brought back again to the Home Office at two o'clock. At half-past two the Council re-assembled, when we understand the prisoner made the following extraordinary statement:—

On Monday night he scaled the wall of Buckingham Palace garden, about half-way up Constitution Hill; he then proceeded to the Palace and effected an entrance through one of the windows. He had not, however, been there long before he considered it unsafe for him to stay, as so many people were moving about, and he left by the same mode as he entered. The next day he again effected an entrance in the same manner as on the previous night; and he went on to state that he remained in the Palace the whole of Tuesday night, the whole day on Wednesday, and up till one o'clock on Thursday morning, when he was discovered under a sofa in her Majesty's dressing-room, as above described. The prisoner pointed out all the passages and places he had gone through previous to his arrival at the room in which he was discovered, and there appears no reason to doubt his statement. The hiding place of the intruder was first discovered by one of her Majesty's pages, and when he was asked what brought him there, he replied, that he wanted to see what was going forward in the Palace, that he might write about it, and if he was discovered he should be as well off as Oxford, who fared better in Bedlam than he (prisoner) did out of it. He was also asked if, during the time he was in the Palace, he saw the Queen or the infant Princess, and he replied that he did not,

but that he had heard a noise, which he thought came from her Majesty's room.

Her Majesty's page, who discovered the prisoner, and the constable who took him to the station-house, were then examined.

The Council came to the decision that, as no property or dangerous weapon was found on the prisoner, it would be better to inflict a summary punishment; and a warrant was accordingly made out, and signed by Mr. Hall, committing the prisoner to the House of Correction, Tothill Street, as a rogue and vagabond, for three months.

The prisoner was immediately afterwards conveyed in a cab to Tothill Street.

LATEST PARTICULARS.

The sensation caused by the late mysterious entrance of the boy Jones into Buckingham Palace, appears to be even greater than that produced by his apprehension in the same place in December, 1838. The object which prompted so daring a proceeding is still involved in the utmost doubt; but it was not probable that it was his intention to do any personal injury to her Majesty, for had such been his purpose abundant opportunities of carrying it into effect presented themselves during his concealment in the chamber where he was secured. From a well informed source, we have heard the sofa under which Jones was found is in the ante-room in which the Princess Royal and Mrs. Lilley, her Royal Highness's nurse, repose. On the night in question the latter had not long retired to rest ere she fancied she heard a noise similar to that likely to be caused by a person who was endeavouring to prevent his presence from being discovered, and was moving in a stealthy manner. Mrs. Lilley, at first treated the matter as of no moment, thinking probably that the noise might have been imaginary. Its renewal, however, created an alarm, and she instantly summoned those of the attendants who were on guard in the adjoining ante-chamber. On their arrival the offender was quickly discovered and drawn from his place of hiding. The statement then goes on to say that her Majesty, who but three hours previously had been sitting on this particular sofa, having been disturbed by the confusion to which the event had given rise, called out and desired to be informed as to its cause. As an apprehension was, however, entertained that the sudden communication of the occurrence might be attended with an unfavourable effect on her Majesty, the attendants gave an evasive answer. The Queen repeated her command, and then the fact of the boy's concealment and subsequent apprehension were made known to her.

The circumstances at that time appeared not to produce any very visible effect on her Majesty, but on Thursday symptoms of other than a satisfactory character were apparent. It affords us the highest gratification to be able to add that a few hours of quietude tended to the restoration of her Majesty.

It would appear that there is now no doubt but that the account given by Jones as to his having effected his entrance into the Palace by scaling the garden wall from Constitution Hill is correct. Upon being asked whether he had not met some of the attendants in the course of his progress along the corridor and staircase, he replied, "Yes," but that, when he saw any one coming in his direction, he hid himself behind the pillars, or behind any piece of furniture which happened to be near. Hitherto he has been silent as to the motive which induced him to take so extraordinary a step as that of forcing his way a second time into the royal apartments, and when asked on Friday morning, after he had been upon the tread-wheel, how he liked his punishment, his answer was to the effect that he had got into the scrape, and must do the best he could.

There does not appear to be the slightest ground for the rumour that he is insane.

Many circumstances have transpired to show that Jones was in the Palace the whole of Wednesday. The delinquent states that during the day he secreted himself under different beds and in cupboards, until at last he obtained an entrance into the room in which he was discovered. Not much reliance can be placed in his statements, but, as such general curiosity exists on the subject, we may state that, in answer to interrogatories, he said, "that he had sat upon the throne, that he saw the Queen, and heard the Princess Royal cry."

Prince Albert was in the room with her Majesty taking leave for the night when the miscreant was discovered under the sofa.

The fellow's shoes were found in one of the rooms of the ground-floor. The sofa under which the boy was discovered, we understand, is one of most costly and magnificent material and workmanship, and ordered expressly for the accommodation of the royal and illustrious visitors who call to pay their respects to her Majesty.

16. The lewdly titled 'A Stranger in Her Majesty's Bedroom!', one of the many catchpenny prints about the Boy Jones affair, reprinted from John Ashton's *Curiosities of Street Literature* (London, 1871). (Author's collection)

17. An interior from Tothill-fields prison. (Author's collection)

18. The entrance to Buckingham Palace, from an old print. (Author's collection)

Top: 19. Buckingham Palace, from vol. 3 of Ackerman's *Microcosm of London.*

Right: 20. Queen Victoria in 1842, an engraving from a miniature in Buckingham Palace by Essex after Winterhalter. (Author's collection)

21. Buckingham Palace from the gardens. Like the following two, this illustration is from vol. 4 of Walford's *Old and New London*. (Author's collection)

22. The King's Library at Buckingham Palace; the Boy Jones was here at least once. (Author's collection)

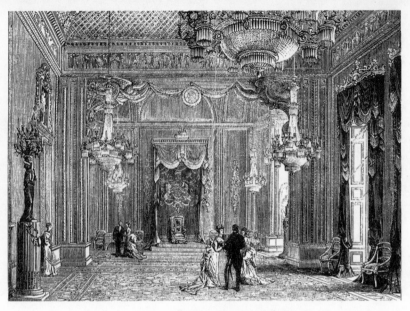

Top: 23. The Throne Room, another regular haunt of the Boy Jones. (Author's collection)

Right: 24. A satirical drawing of the Boy Jones spying on the Queen and Prince, from the cover of 'The Boy wot visits the Palace', a comic song by James Bruton. (From the private collection of Mr Michael Diamond, reproduced by permission)

CHIT-CHAT.

only things which we rise from reading this President's message without getting any information at all about. Harrison appears as much afraid of mentioning the name of M'Leod as his Satanic Majesty would be afraid of mentioning the name of his old enemy the Archangel, who gave him that ugly cut from chin to chine, which Milton was present at and witnessed—at least we suppose he was, for he gives as accurate an account of it as a penny-a-liner would of a fire in a mur cred man's throat. M'Leod's name is never once mentioned in the message; and, instead of talking over all the difficulties between his country and England, like a sensible man, he apes the language of the regal puppets of Europe, and tells us that the "foreign relations" are all right, because he is sure that none of them will ask anything which it would be courteous in the honour of America to grant.

We are not quite so sure of this. If America chooses to spit in our face, or to kick us in the rear, the least she can expect is to knuckle down upon her murderousness and to make an apology, or else to feel our John Bull fist making her teeth fly down her throat. If she lays hold of our countryman, and throws him into a prison, with a polite intimation that in a short time he will be led out to be hanged, the least she can expect is that we shall burn enough of her towns to make her a handsome illumination in order to commemorate her exploit. If she chooses to send all her vagabonds to take possession of our territory, the best she can expect is that we shall clear our lands of incumbrances, just as the Americans clear their forests. Where she may put her honour, or what she may consider her honour to require, we don't know; but we beg to assure old Harrison, that if he does not very soon cry peccavi, and promise never to do so any more, it is not at all impossible but that we may bring him some fine morning over to England, and show him at a shilling a head.

Nobody seems to know what is to be done with M'Leod. The newspapers say little or nothing about him; the President never mentions his name. All we hear is that he is still in prison expecting his trial, and that it is probable that he will be removed from where he now is to some more secure prison. We beg leave to ask why the Ministers have not taken our hint last week? Why have they not seized some hostages for the safety of this man? Why did they not lay hold of Mr. Biddle, whom we pointed out to them, or some other American, known in his own country? and why don't they make arrangements for hanging up their hostage at the first moment that they hear of the murder of any English prisoner, be he M'Leod, or anybody else?

In contradiction to the report about the Princess Royal being blind, it has been stated that she "can see the smallest object in life;" the hope is, from this, that she may be taught in due season to see herself!

When Twiss was told that the boy Jones "got in" through the kitchen window, he ran off to Peel as fast as his legs would carry him to suggest that he and his friends should get in by the same way. Horace particularly making an offer of his services to be leader in the business!

Mrs. Mountjoy Martyn has had a strange freak of late, and has left off indulging in Reid's Entire! Her delicate stomach and improved taste cannot bear the heavy wet.

THE ROYAL CREED.

(To be said and sung in all Palaces.)

Italian music, German imposture,
English artistes i' the regions not cold i
Foreign bedvestments—keed not their coat sure—
And one only thing English—pure English gold i

The learned parrot cannot understand how it is that the boy Jones should be no anxious to get into the Palace, when her most anxious wish is, and always has been, to get out of it i

It has been recommended by a certain Lord of the Bedchamber that the Red Duchess should, to insure what she is most desirous to possess, try the air of Torrington-square. The advice will, no doubt, be joyfully taken.

"Do you know, Polly," quoth the Queen to the learned parrot, referring to the visit of the boy Jones, "that there has been another intruder found in my Palace?" "Ah, your Majesty," exclaimed the sagacious bird, "'tis my wondering about this vast house, the other day, I lighted by accident upon a stray volume of plays written by one William Shakspere, in which he speaks of 'that Palace wherein foul things intrude not.' Had the poet written in these days, he would have left out the last word."

LOCAL ASSOCIATIONS.

Saint Mary-le-Strand lies in the Strand,
By Somerset-house you'll find her i
Saint Clement the Dane stands near at hand,
Within a short space behind her.
But in this remark there is nothing at all,
Save only 'twas made by Marian Wall i

When Melbourne heard that the boy Jones had helped himself to some of the Palace mutton, he was most curious to know the joint of which he partook, and which, upon inquiry, turned out not to be a leg, as at first supposed, but a slice that was placed on the shelf between two legs, and which, being cut to his hand, he appropriated without hesitation.

While we are expending millions to establish colonies abroad, the lousy Germans are establishing colonies here, and sending over shiploads of unwashed, shirtless, shoeless vagabonds to engender filth in our streets and houses. The Drury-Lane colony of itinerant singers and fiddlers has already become a nuisance to the neighbourhood, and the stench of garlic and train oil is not to be endured. The imperial town is purity itself, and a nosegay, compared with the lodging room of a German. What must be the air of an ill-ventilated apartment with two beds and four German brutes in them, we leave our readers to guess.

PRINCE GARDE.

Young Paul Pry, who, the other day,
(From curiosity, not malice,)
In cap, beneath the sofa lay
In Buckingham's male-guarded Palace.
When ask'd if he was not in fear
Of gracious Newgate gallows?
Replied, "He had so much right there
Within the Royal Palace,
As Lamb had all his sheepish set.
Had in the Royal Cabinet i

The Palace footmen are prohibited entering the Royal nursery, from the circumstance of its being represented to the Queen that the Princess Royal, in her childish innocence, mistook one of them for her Royal parent i

Lady Abingdon says she cannot conceive what women get married for; a remark that leads to the inference that her noble lord has failed to convince her of the importance of matrimonial obligations i

There is not a word of truth in the report that Castlereagh is going to be married; or if indeed he is, it must be, as Rogers says, because he has been going for some time i

THE FALSE MAN.

"Should Palmerston go off some day,"
Quoth Poll, at Albert nodding,
"How handed will he then, I say,
Be found, poor soul, with wadding."

"I suppose," said an old friend to Lord Abingdon in the presence of the new bride, "you have been keeping it up finely since your marriage?" "O, no; I assure you he has not, indeed," replied Lady A., "he has been particularly quiet i"

It is absurd for people to say the Princess Royal is blind; the blindness is on the part of the people i

The Queen and Prince Albert pass a good deal of their time, it is said, in the Royal nursery—we should think so by their adroitness in nursing John Bull i

A BUG AT ROYALTY BY ROYAL POLL.
To patronise all that's not English won't do,
Or the English will cease soon to patronise you i

The law officers of the Crown are cudgelling their brains to strain the law so as to secure the boy Jones seven years' transportation. This is all the urchin requires; particularly if it be that kind of transportation that he experienced during his visit to the Palace larder.

"You cut a bad figure in the House, the other night," said the vice-Countess to her Hope lord. "A bad figure?" iterated the noble Secretary, "I cut my coat according to my cloth." "That's true enough," replied the lady, "but not according to the last new shape."

"SOMETHING FROM THE PALACE."

"An English waistkit! I'm shocked!" cries the cries.
"The vulgar thing i will not patronize."

As the urchin intruder in the Palace, young Jones, in a letter to his father, stated that his reason for entering the Queen's house was to "seek for some in order to rite a book," it is a matter of general regret that, instead of magnifying the affair into Home-office importance, the young rogue was not accommodated with a rope's end.

The boy Jones is of opinion that if in his rambles through the palace, he could only have "come across" the Queen, he should have been provided for for life. There is no doubt, we think, about the matter.

GOOD FOR THE HEALTH.
"I want a change of air, my dear"—
Her Grace will ramble on.
"A change!" exclaimed the "dotard" peer,
"Then go to Torrington i"

Appended to the "Wand Demon," the "Lady and the Devil," "Solmons," the "Assassin," and numerous other dramatic horrors, is a significant note, editorially placed, calling upon the reader to "ask for Cumberland's edition."

The urchin Jones, to a question put by the Master of the Household, during the boy's examination at the Home-office, remarked that if he entered the Palace with dirty feet (his shoes being stated to be covered with mud), he appeared in Court with clean hands, and that was more than could be said of every person present i

MELBOURNE'S DINNER CREED.
When out he dines at home: he's wise, no doubt;
When in his creed is always to dine out i

Alfred Paget lost his bet the other day that "Torrington was in Somerset," by neglecting the necessary proof of the affirmative of what he had advanced.

The joke is in the Clubs that if Lord Graves "found his lady out," he was not so unfortunate in regard to her musical instructor; for it is clear enough that he found him in i

A LESSON FOR THE TORIES.
Ha! ha! grinned young Jones at some dull Tory wranglers,
You see I well know the right end to begin;
While you prowl about after Peel, as his danglers,
I by a bold step contrive to get in i

Baring Wall's friends account for his going over to the Whigs, on the score of the gentlemen of that party always paying him more respect than the Tories, by giving him precedence on every possible occasion i

Londonderry complains bitterly of the Marchioness of late, that on every intimation of his desire to fulfil his marital pledge, his lady "puts him off," preferring, as she says, to be without attentions which fail in their avowed object, and are as nothing in the intent and purpose of their fulfilment i

A ROYAL QUERY.
"If Jones can get in," quoth the deep thinking Queen,
Who considers each Tory a bore i;
"How the deuce—tell me, Mel, seeing what we have seen,
Can we much longer keep out the Tories?"

If, as some would infer, it was a mistake on the part of Eglinton to marry the widow Cockerell, if we consider the wealth of the lady no one will venture to say, we think, that it was a mis-fortune.

D'Israeli asserts that it is a convincing proof of his being no Jew, the fact of his being seen so much in company with his friend Hogg.

"Shall I scratch a pole, Polly," asked Victoria of the parrot. "No," replied the sarcastic bird; "scratch a German, who is much more likely to require scratching than a Pole, any day."

THE ROYAL LARDER.
"Jones seized the Queen's mutton; how lucky I am."
Exclaimed Melbourne, "the rascal did not seize her Lamb."

A friend of Lady Dinorben asked if her husband placed ful confidence in her, and trusted to her all his affairs? "He has put every thing into my hands," was Gertrude's reply, "but nothing has been done at present."

The boy Jones, from his extraordinary powers of finding an entrance into Buckingham Palace, must be, says Sam Rogers, a descendant of the illustrious In-i-go.

25. Two columns from the *Satirist* of 28 March 1841, containing a total of thirteen Boy Jones puns or verses. (Author's collection)

26. The Sweep in the Palace, a caricature from the *Sunday Chronicle* of 4 April 1841. (Author's collection)

OLD HARRY'S VISIT TO JONES, IN SEARCH OF USEFUL KNOWLEDGE.

" Now, my lad, just inform me how you managed to *get in*, for that's the very thing *I want to do !* '
' Vy, yer see, my Lord, I can't wery well do that, 'cos I means to go back again ven I gets out o' quod.'

27. Old Harry's visit to Jones, a caricature from the *Odd Fellow* of 24 April 1841, depicting the Boy giving some advice to politician 'Old Harry' Brougham. The Boy Jones may well have been drawn from life. (Author's collection)

28. *A Peep into the Palace*, from Catalogue 169 of Jarndyce Booksellers. (Reproduced by permission)

Bottom: 29. 'The Three Jones-es; Or, Spies in the Palace'. A satirical drawing depicting the Duke of Wellington and two ministerial colleagues invading Buckingham Palace after the Tory election win, from the *Penny Satirist*, 4 September 1841. (Author's collection)

Left: 30. The satirical print 'A Soliloquy' by John Doyle, depicting Lord Melbourne, who had only twice been Prime Minister, exclaiming, 'That boy Jones must be a very clever fellow. To make his way into the palace once or twice was not so extraordinary. I have done as much as that myself, but how he contrived to get in the third time! I wish I knew his secret.' (Author's collection)

Right: 31. The Boy Jones as a sailor, a fanciful drawing from *Punch*, 27 July 1844. (Author's collection)

Below: 32. An excerpt from the official record of the second and third entries of the Boy Jones from the official police memorandum about individuals who posed dangers to royalty, PRO MEPO 2/44. The last entry concerns his desertion from the *Warspite*. (Reproduced by permission of the National Archives, Kew)

RETURN OF THE BOY JONES;
OR, THE WHIG JONESES AND THEIR LEADER.

33. 'Return of the Boy Jones; Or, the Whig Joneses and their Leader'. Another drawing from the *Penny Satirist*, 5 November 1842, this time representing the Boy himself leading Lord Melbourne and his Whig ministers back into the palace. The unflattering countenance of the Boy is said to have been a good likeness. (Author's collection)

OLD PEARHEAD'S VISIT TO THE WINDSOR PAIR.

LOUIS PHILIPPE—Ah! my spliced pair, my jolis chers enfans! what a compliment to the *Père* of France! How I long to embrace de pair of you! My hair apperent stands on end with delight at de sight of my little Mistress of de Sees. Oh! I have brought such presents for you—a picture book for my little Queen, and a pair of powder-horns for the sovereign of her heart, a foul-ing piece for de Prangse of Gals (French for Wales).

JONES *(behind the pair)*—He has got a pretty good foul ing piece already.

LOUIS PHILIPPE *(not having heard Jones)*—And dolls for the Prangsesses, dressed by my mantuamaker, cigar-cases and spit-boxes for de Ministers of de State, snuff-boxes for de Gentlemen of de Household, pincushions and thimblerigs for de Ladies, brooms with gilt handles for de Housemaids, and kisses from all de Gentlemen and Ladies of France to all de Gentlemen and Ladies of England. Oh! dis happy day! It makes my old bones as fresh as a greenhorn. France and England in marriage union for ever! Diss is de consummation! Pare and Peel!

N.B.—Louis Philippe's head resembles a pear in shape. The French caricatured it as a pear till a prosecution put an end to the innocent drollery. His Majesty cannot bear to be laughed at, and has officially interdicted the admission of the PENNY SATIRIST into his dominions. However, we send it sometimes by post.

34. A caricature of the Boy Jones spying on King Louis Philippe of France being received by Queen Victoria and Prince Albert, from the *Penny Satirist*, 19 October 1844. (Author's collection)

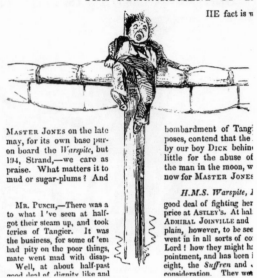

MASTER JONES on the late
may, for its own base pur-
on board the *Warspite*, but
194, Strand,—we care as
praise. What matters it to
mud or sugar-plums? And

MR. PUNCH,—There was a
to what I've seen at half-
got their steam up, and took
teries of Tangier. It was
the business, for some of 'em
had pity on the poor things,
mate went mad with disap-

Well, at about half-past
good deal of dignity like and

bombardment of Tang
poses, contend that the
by our boy DICK behind
little for the abuse of
the man in the moon, w
now for MASTER JONES

H.M.S. Warspite, l
good deal of fighting her
price at ASTLEY'S. At hal
ADMIRAL JOINVILLE and
plain, however, to be see
went in in all sorts of co
Lord! how they might h:
pointment, and has been i
eight, the *Suffren* and
consideration. They we

35. The Boy Jones
clinging to the mast
of his ship during
the bombardment
of Tangiers, another
fanciful drawing from
Punch, 31 August 1844.
(Author's collection)

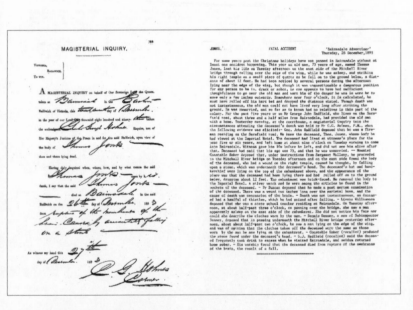

36. The Magisterial Inquiry into the death of Thomas Jones in Bairnsdale, December
1893, reproduced by permission of the East Gippsland Historical Society.

REYNOLDS'S MISCELLANY
Of Romance, General Literature, Science, and Art.
EDITED BY GEORGE W. M. REYNOLDS,
AUTHOR OF "THE MYSTERIES OF LONDON," "FAUST," "MASTER TIMOTHY'S BOOK-CASE," &c.

No. 1. Vol. I.   SATURDAY, NOVEMBER 7, 1846.   Price 1d.

MR. GEORGE W. M. REYNOLDS.

WAGNER: THE WEHR-WOLF.
BY THE EDITOR.

PROLOGUE.

It was the month of January, 1516. The night was dark and tempestuous;—the thunder growled around;—the lightning flashed at short inter-vals—and the wind swept furiously along, in sudden and fitful gusts.

The streams of the great Black Forest of Germany bubbled in playful melody no more, but rushed on with deafening din, mingling their torrent-roar with the wild creaking of the huge oaks, the rustling of the firs, the howling of the affrighted wolves, and the hollow voices of the storm.

The dense black clouds were driving restlessly athwart

37. George W. R. Reynolds, a portrait from his *Reynolds's Miscellany*, 1846. (Author's collection)

38. The Resurrection Man plies his trade. Like the following five, this illustration is from an early edition of *The Mysteries of London* by G. W. R. Reynolds. (Author's collection)

Top, right, and next page: 39. Some more or less lewd engravings from *The Mysteries of London*. (Author's collection)

40. The pot-boy Henry Holford is helped over the wall to Buckingham Palace by the Resurrection Man and the Cracksman. (Author's collection)

41. Hidden underneath the sofa just like the Boy Jones, Henry Holford spies on Queen Victoria and Prince Albert. (Author's collection)

42. Having again entered Buckingham Palace, Holford spies on Queen Victoria and Prince Albert. (Author's collection)

43. The demented Holford fires a pistol at the Queen and Prince. (Author's collection)

44. The jolly-looking Boy Jones larking about in Buckingham Palace, one of the drawings from Patricia Gordon's *The Boy Jones*. (Author's collection)

45. The Boy Jones at sea, another drawing from Patricia Gordon's book. (Author's collection)

46. Michael Fagan, from the cover of his record. (Author's collection)

47. A still from *Jones* the musical, reproduced by permission of Mr Peter Gritton and the mother of the actor depicted.

had come into the cigar rooms, where he sat at a table, silently grinning at the Boy Jones. Fearful that he would be abducted again, Edward asked Mr Elgar to be employed indoors, and not sent out on any errands. The tobacconist, who had himself not seen anything suspicious, thought that young Edward's imagination was running away with him, but nevertheless acceded to the Boy's working indoors for a while. On Friday morning, 4 February, Edward again saw the 'midshipman' following him to the Tothill-street tobacconist's shop. He asked Mr Elgar's permission to return home, which was granted. He made it all the way home, where he requested his mother to give him a clean shirt. At between 10 and 11 in the morning, he again left home, but never arrived at the tobacconist's. Nor did he return home.

Reeling at this latest in the never-ending series of disasters that had overtaken his family, poor Henry Jones 'suffered the greatest anxiety and distress of mind'. He scoured the streets of London looking for his son, and visited the various police offices, but without finding Edward or obtaining any worthwhile clues. But on Monday 7 February, Henry Jones received a mysterious letter dated two days earlier, with a Winchester postmark:

Sir,

I am requested by your son Edward to inform you he has sailed on board the ____, for America, on Friday last, he not being satisfied with his last place, and sends his *cloth* to you, and wishes you to remember him to his old and faithful friend, Mr James.

I remain, a Captain, and Well-wisher to your son.

The receipt of this short and ominous letter did nothing to alleviate Henry Jones's anxiety for his son. He knew that Edward had in fact been very pleased with his work at Mr Elgar's shop, and that after his dismal experiences with the brutal Captain Taylor and his crew, he had always expressed great aversion to going back to sea. And why had the ship's name been omitted? Nor was the perfidious Mr James exactly a trusted friend of the family; in fact, the mentioning of his name seemed to imply that some further villainy was afoot.

It turned out that Mr Elgar had also received a mysterious letter, bearing the Portsmouth postmark, and the date 6 February 1842:

Dear Sir,

About the 1st of February my Father informed me that Mr. James, Proprietor of the Bell, in Westminster, had informed him that a gentleman had sent a Letter to Mr. James, explaining his wish to give me a good Sittiation at Sea; that Mr. James had Returned an answer Declaring that I was Provided with a good Sittiation; that I was Sickened with the Sea, and therefore he (Mr. James) would not act in the affair. However, I went to Mr. James, and after Conversing with him, I entreated him to write to his Friends that I was desirous to be aware of the nature of his offers. Mr. James then Promised to write the following time, at wich I went to Mr. James, I was introduced to his Frend, who informed me that the Captain was a kind Gentleman, and if I was determined on Entering his Service, I should act as Cabin-boy or Servant …

When Henry Jones read this curious missive, with its many lapses in spelling and grammar, he declared that it was definitely in Edward's handwriting. But what a strange letter! Its stilted phrases seemed to hint that some person had dictated its contents to poor Edward, who had to spell the difficult words as well as he could.[7]

In the letter, the Boy went on to explain that, on extremely short notice, he had gone on to accept this offer. The very same afternoon, he was transported down to Portsmouth in a great hurry, and the next morning he was all at sea again, on board the *Warspite*, a fifty-two-gun frigate under the command of Captain Lord John Hay, on the way to New York. Mr James's friend, who had escorted Edward to Portsmouth, provided him with a naval uniform and told him that he was now 'on board to serve four yeeres or more as a Seaman'. The mysterious letter ended with these cryptic and surreal phrases:

> While I was Writing this Letter a Boy informed me that Mr. Loyd, a Midshipman, inquired whether my name was E or Abraham; the boy said 'You know him, don't you!' I answered in the affirmative the boy. He said 'Do you want to see him?' I inquired wether he sent for. The boy said 'No.' I then said 'Never mind.' I then inquired wether he was a Midshipman of the Ship, and wether Mr. Loyd was to accompany the ship. He answered in the affirmative. I am surprised to hear this, as Mr. Loyd is the said Frend of Mr. James, and who shook hands with me as I entered the *Warspite*'s boat. Give my kind Respects to my Parents, Sisters, and brothers. I have told Mr J. to settle the 8s. you advanced. Farewell.
> Edwin Jones

Poor Henry Jones went to the Home Office, humbly asking what it intended to do about his son, but although he appeared much anxious and excited, he received the curt reply that since there was no inquiry into this matter ongoing, no answer could be given. Since, according to his letter, the Boy Jones had joined the navy from his own free will, nothing could or should be done about him.

So, what can be deduced, from the evidence available, about the second mysterious disappearance of the Boy Jones? A benign view would be that the Boy suddenly changed his mind for some reason and decided to join the Royal Navy. Maybe he had had enough of life in London, where everybody recognised him as the notorious In-I-Go Jones; maybe he had become tired of his boring job at the tobacconist's shop and wanted to become a jolly Jack

Tar and serve his country on the ocean wave. But there are many arguments against this theory. Both Henry Jones and Mr Elgar agreed that Edward had greatly abhorred the idea of going back to sea after being so badly treated during his voyage to Brazil and back. And the Royal Navy was known for its hard work and strict discipline. And surely, if Edward had really decided to join the navy, he would have told his parents about this decision rather than just dashing off into the night; after all, his mother had always been very fond of her eldest son, and his father had borrowed heavily to keep him out of prison. And when men joined the Royal Navy in these days, they were usually first posted to some training ship or other establishment to be taught the rudiments of seamanship. They were certainly not bundled on board a ship destined for the United States the very next day, with hardly the time to be provided with a suitable uniform. It has to be suspected that some exalted person had decided that, in order to protect Queen Victoria from her bothersome stalker, the Boy Jones once more had to be forcibly removed from London.

It is very likely that the same group of individuals who arranged the first abduction of the Boy Jones were again conspiring against him. It would seem as if their main agent once more was the perfidious Mr James, who kept spying on the Boy and his family, this time aided by his 'Frend' Midshipman Loyd. It must be suspected that these two worthies abducted the Boy in London and that the midshipman took him to Portsmouth post-haste. The fact that the *Warspite*, the ship to which Loyd belonged, sailed for America the very next morning, would indicate that the abduction of the Boy was a preconceived plan, aiming to remove Edward from his friends in London. Captain Lord John Hay was the son of the Marquess of Tweeddale and had served as a Member of Parliament in the 1820s. With his aristocratic connections and loyalty to the government, he would have been the ideal person to swear into such a conspiracy. Midshipman Loyd or some other person had probably dictated the letter to Edward, who had struggled to spell some of the long and unfamiliar words, but he had still been clever enough to sign his name Edwin instead of Edward to try to alert his elderly parent that further villainy was afoot.

The anti-Jones newspapers were very pleased the notorious Boy was gone once more, and the Queen free from her stalker, whereas the pro-Jones faction hinted at dark government conspiracies against the hapless Boy. *The Times* wrote that 'suspicion strongly points to the same parties who rendered themselves so notoriously conspicuous in his former abduction; and though the father of the boy is in such reduced circumstances as to be unable to take legal measures; it is probable means may be found to fathom this mysterious matter'.[8] The jolly *Satirist* wrote that since another entrance of the Boy Jones would mean a prompt discharge for some of the head 'gentlemen' of the palace, these senior courtiers had spared neither pains nor money to spirit him out of the country once more. For contriving to see a little too much *at home*, the Boy had been sent for a voyage of discovery *abroad*![9]

The log and muster book of the *Warspite* tells us that the unwilling sailor Edward Jones crossed the Atlantic, serving as a second-class ship's boy. Possibly he was one of the servants of the captain, Lord John Hay. In New York, the ship delivered Lord Ashburton, a former government minister who was to negotiate a border treaty between Canada and the United States. This having been the only objective of the cruise, the ship sailed back to Portsmouth straight away. The Boy's conduct was said to have been good throughout this voyage. On 22 May 1842, he was promoted to first-class boy. In the ship's muster book, he is described as being aged nineteen years (he was really just eighteen), born in the parish of Westminster, London, Middlesex. He was stated to be a carpenter by trade, 5 feet 4 inches in height, complexion fair, eyes blue, no marks on person, vaccinated, single.[10] Since he was a good and willing climber, he was made mizentopmast-man and carried out his hazardous duties to everyone's satisfaction, or so at least it was alleged.

In early October 1842, the *Warspite* was finally back in Portsmouth. Since Lord John Hay was well aware of the instructions from Lord Auckland, the First Lord of the Admiralty, he ordered that the Boy Jones was to be strictly watched by his shipmates and by Midshipman Loyd to prevent him from escaping to London. Edward's conduct remained exemplary, however. When some of the other sailors went on shore, Edward was allowed to accompany them, under Loyd's supervision. Since the Boy had been paid regular wages of 19 shillings per month during his time as a seaman, he had money to spend. When he went into a shop, Loyd and the others waited for a while, but Edward did not emerge. When the suspicious midshipman barged into the shop asking for him, all the shopkeeper could say was that the young sailor had asked him whether there was a back door to the shop and then swiftly made use of it! The frantic Midshipman divided his men into search parties, scouring the Portsmouth streets, but all these impromptu press gangs could capture was a man wearing Edward' sailor's jacket, which he said he had recently purchased from a sailor boy, giving his own old black coat and 4 shillings for it.[11]

The distraught Midshipman Loyd dashed back to the *Warspite* to report that the Boy Jones had given him the slip. Belatedly, Lord John Hay must have regretted that the Boy had not been more strictly guarded and that the foolish Midshipman Loyd had allowed him to go on shore. Because of this bungling youth, Lord John was in immediate danger of becoming a laughing stock within his own profession, for setting the notorious Boy Jones at liberty to plan novel outrages. Queen Victoria's stalker, the state prisoner who had been put under his care and surveillance, was on the prowl and free to strike again. Due to his successful stratagem of changing his garments, it seemed unlikely the shore patrol or local police would be able to apprehend him. Nobody had any idea in which direction the Boy Jones had left Portsmouth, but Lord John must have had an unpleasant feeling that, with the instinct of a homing pigeon, Queen Victoria's stalker was on his way back to Buckingham Palace.

Lord John Hay sent two of his officers to London post-haste to warn the Queen and the Home Secretary that the Boy Jones had escaped. Since everyone involved seems to have been sworn to secrecy, the newspapers cannot inform us about how the establishment reacted to this threat. It would appear as if the police presence at Buckingham Palace was greatly reinforced, like if a conquering army were working its way northwards from Portsmouth, rather than a young boy in a shabby black coat. Reliable police agents were posted near Henry Jones's hovel in Bell-yard, at Mr Elgar's cigar shop, and at other places they thought the Boy might be likely to visit. But days and weeks went by without any sighting of the Boy. Like in a present-day terrorist scare, the 'threat level' was gradually reduced.

Early in the morning of 18 October 1842, the police inspector on duty at the Gardener's-lane station house was woken by the persistent ringing of Mr James, the Judas of Bell-yard, who breathlessly reported that the Boy Jones had just been sighted at his father's hovel. A party of constables was immediately dispatched to this address and the Boy taken into custody. Since he had been on the road for several weeks after leaving Portsmouth, Edward expressed surprise and dismay that the police had been able to recapture him so very swiftly. Fearing that Midshipman Loyd and his boatswains were after him, he had not dared to travel by train or coach, but tramped all the way to London. His journey had been full of hardships. A lifelong Londoner with a very limited knowledge of geography, his sense of direction had often failed him; he had been at the mercy of the mischievous country yokels, who had given him erroneous directions. Having walked round in circles for many days, the footsore Boy had finally regained his bearings and started to make headway back to London. There had been further adventures along the way: once he had been stopped and questioned by a police constable, but managed to keep a straight face. When sleeping in a barn, he had been robbed of his handkerchief, purse and cap by another vagabond.

When the police inspector asked him why he had escaped back to London, the Boy replied that the other sailors had often treated him unkindly. Everybody knew he was none other than the Boy Jones, of Buckingham Palace notoriety, and he was heartily tired of all the jokes at his expense. Although the police constables who knew him thought his appearance had improved, remarking that he had grown quite corpulent, the Boy seemed apathetic and extremely depressed. He did not care what was done with him, he said, even if he was taken back to the *Warspite*. He did not dislike a seafaring life, preferring it to a prison. He was taken to the station house in Gardener's-lane, where he amused himself by reading an old newspaper and making the occasional facetious remark. A police officer was sent to the Home Office to report that the Boy Jones had been recaptured, and after a few hours, a messenger came back with a government order that the Boy was to be sent back to Portsmouth with the greatest expedition. The reason for this was probably to avoid further newspaper speculation. Since there was no need for any police inquiry, it would be left to the officers of the *Warspite* to punish the fugitive sailor in their customary manner. Accordingly, a police constable conveyed the Boy on board the South West Express the very same evening, to be delivered into the hands of Lord John Hay of the *Warspite*.[11] It is not known exactly what happened to the Boy Jones when he was returned to his ship, but it is unlikely that Midshipman Loyd and his boatswains treated the deserter particularly kindly.

In the press, the reaction to these latest events was characteristically mixed. The *Examiner* exclaimed that what water is to the parched traveller, the Boy Jones is to the newspapers.[12] Once more he had turned up to refresh their columns, although this time he had been stopped short of reaching the palace: 'He is the cricket-ball of her Majesty's servants guarding the wicket of the Palace. Lord Melbourne, in his innings, had hard work to block him out. We shall see whether Sir Robert Peel is a better bat.' The jolly *Satirist* wrote that it was clear that royalty and the Boy Jones could not coexist.[13] Either her Majesty must abdicate or the Boy be sent abroad: 'So great is the terror which his repeated incursions into the Palace have inspired, that our beloved Queen cannot feel herself in safety unless the "boy" is removed far off, and oceans roll between him and royalty.' The only good news to come out of the Boy's flying visit to the Metropolis was that, according to the newspapers, he had grown quite corpulent, meaning that he could no longer sneak through the Buckingham Palace nooks and crannies.

The *John Bull* was one of the few papers to sound a critical note. After announcing that the Boy Jones was back, 'Like a re-appearing star/Like a glory from afar', the newspaper actually felt some pity for the involuntary sailor who had been treated so very harshly: 'Really, when we read this, we feel quite *desorienté*. Are we in England, or in Russia? Poor Jones was guilty only of displaying some refined tastes – some glorious aspirations.' When the celebrated female Chartist Mary Anne Walker gave a speech in London and ridiculed those who sought notoriety so much that they flung themselves from the top of the Monument, or 'forced themselves into the Queen's Palace', *John Bull* again took up the cudgel for the Boy Jones: 'It is strange Miss Walker has not a tear to shed, or a sigh to breathe for the sad fate of the boy Jones, or an indignant reclamation to hurl against a heartless executive for the illegal and unconstitutional treatment to which he has been subjected. If Jones had been an American, Mr Dickens would have devoted a whole pathetic and philanthropic chapter to his case.'[14] And indeed, in his *Miscellaneous Papers*, Charles Dickens did question whether a young boy could really be considered so very dangerous that such extreme measures had to be taken to keep him at bay, speaking ironically about 'the wisdom of the Boy Jones precedent, of kidnapping such youths after the expiration of their several terms of imprisonment as vagabonds; hurrying them on board ship; and packing them off to sea again whenever they venture to take the air on shore'.

7

Britain's Galley Slave

The Boy Jones sent to sea

Jones, you'll be toss'd at sea, as I've a notion;
But the dread perils of the sea, O shun!
Winds, when the fair Aurora dawns, O roar
Not in your might till Jones has gone ashore;
Waters, swell not yon yeasty billows high,
Till that young swell's on land, and very dry;
For though his name *is* Jones, and though he did
Enter the Palace, and not touch the knocker,
There is no reason why Jones's kid
Should be consigned to Davy Jones's locker.

From the *Comic Almanack* for 1842

After his dramatic escape and recapture in October 1842, we hear little about the Boy Jones and his life afloat for a number of months. The *Warspite* was based at Gibraltar, and the days were mostly passed in routine exercise: washing down ship, sail drill, cutlass drill and cannon drill. Discipline was harsh and floggings were frequent. But still, the Boy Jones was not to be kept quiet for long. On a fine night in early 1844, the *Warspite* was cruising between Tunis and Algiers. Suddenly, there was a loud shout of 'Man overboard!' Quite a few of the officers and seamen were still awake, and they immediately sprung into action. Both first and second cutters were away, and the lifebuoy was also made use of. Although the sea was not very rough, the buoy dropped considerably astern. When the cutters reached it, the seamen were amazed to see the Boy Jones holding on to it with one hand, dashing the sparks of the port-fire away from his face with the other and hollering, 'Here I am, look lively!' He was dragged into one of the cutters, the other taking the buoy in tow.

When questioned by the lieutenant of the watch, Jones said he had fallen out of the mizzen rigging accidentally. But the ship's crew all believed that he had deliberately jumped overboard. One of them claimed to have heard him shouting 'Man overboard!' himself when in mid-air, and later, when immersed, 'Let go the lifebuoy!' When reproached for this rash and dangerous act, the Boy was as taciturn as ever and revealed nothing. The sailors thought the mischievous Boy Jones had jumped overboard just to see the lifebuoy light burning. One of the ship's officers, who wrote about the incident to a friend back in England found this explanation not unlikely, since he knew the Boy as 'a singular character'. Still, risking one's life for such a meagre reward seems foolhardy indeed. There is no record of the Boy Jones attempting suicide, even when his fortunes were at their lowest ebb, and if it had been his purpose to destroy himself, he would hardly have shouted to alert his shipmates, or clung to the lifebuoy. It might well have been an attempt to escape that failed through want of courage and/or ability to swim. As a punishment, the first lieutenant stopped four of the eight dollars the Boy was to be paid, but when told the reason, the Boy 'burst into a great passion, and flung the remaining four dollars into the sea.'[1]

The newspapers avidly picked up this first snippet of news about the Boy Jones.[2] A parsimonious journalist commented that he should have been more harshly punished for his abnormal curiosity about lifebuoys, which had led to the light of the buoy being wastefully burnt. What if he would next want to find out about the ship's powder magazine and blow his shipmates sky high? Other newspaper men were more concerned about some proposed changes to the censorship laws, ribaldly suggesting that, with his inordinate curiosity, the Boy Jones should be employed by the Home Secretary as chief letter-opener. His old friends at the *Satirist* facetiously presumed that the intention of Boy Jones's dangerous midnight bath in the Mediterranean must have been that he intended to visit 'the submarine palace of the monarch of the wave, for the purpose of prying into the coral chamber of Neptune and Amphitrite.'

In early December 1844, when the *Warspite* was anchored off Athens, the Boy Jones made another attempt to escape.[3] This time, he successfully swam ashore, but since his shipmates continued to keep an eye on his activities, a search party swiftly followed. According to one of the officers of the *Warspite*, the sailors had been joking that the Boy Jones had probably 'gone to see King Otho. I believe that was his intention, since he was found near the Palace, and brought back very much disappointed to think he could not pay his intended visit. He is a strange-looking fellow, appears half asleep, and seldom speaks to any one.' For this escapade, the Boy was put on the black list and had his grog stopped for as long as he would remain on board the *Warspite*. Again, the Boy's latest adventures were jocularly related by the newspapers home in England; they queried whether he might perchance have sneaked into King Otho's palace to escape the press gang pursuing him.[4]

By the mid-1840s, several other humorous newspapers had established themselves in London. Both the *Penny Satirist* and the *New Satirist* took the Boy Jones to their hearts.[5] With its usual 'below the belt' humour, the *New Satirist* imagined what the examination of the Boy Jones before the Privy Council had been like:

> 'When you were under the sofa at the Palace, and the Queen and Prince were sitting upon it, what did you hear?' demanded Mr Hall, the magistrate, of the boy Jones, during the examination at the Home Office. 'Why, at first,' answered the urchin, with a leer, 'the Queen was inclined to be angry about something; but the Prince was determined to get over her, and so he did. What is all I can say about the matter.'

The *Penny Satirist* had vague pro-Jones sentiments and once expressed its outrage that he had been 'kidnapped by the police, and pressed on board a man-of-war, in violation of all law'. One of its regular features was 'The Boy Jones's Court Circular', in which it was imagined that the Boy had escaped from his captivity on board ship and again visited the Queen at Buckingham Palace. This ribald serial usually began with the words 'The Queen was in the chair. The boy Jones was under it.' Once, it was imagined that 'her Majesty saw the snake's eyes of the boy Jones peeping out from beneath an ottoman. She screamed, and the Countess screamed, and the boy Jones made his escape nobody knows how.' In another issue, the Queen had an angry quarrel with Prince Albert, ending that 'the Prince timidly withdrew, and her Majesty fell into fits. But the boy Jones most opportunely crept out from below a sofa, and, taking a handkerchief dipped in water, gently wiped her brow. This, however, did not suffice; and he filled up a tumbler with the crystal fluid, which he dashed into her face and disappeared ...'

The early issues of *Punch* are also full of the real and imaginary exploits of the Boy Jones.[6] In an article on Buckingham Palace, it was commented that the ante-room to the Queen's bedroom was also called 'The Boy Jones's Room', since this dignitary had hitherto been its principal occupant. In 'The Boy Jones's Log', the seafaring hero himself tells his strange story, in weird cockney parlance:

> Halass, Sir, the wicktim of that crewel bluebeard, Lord Melbun, who got affeard of my rising popularity in the Palass, and as sent me to *see* for my *peeping*, though, heaven nose, I was acktyated by the pewrest motifs in what I did. The reel fex of the case is, I'm a young man of an ighly cultiwated mind and a very *ink*-wisitive disposition, which naturally led me to the use of my *pen*.

The Boy was planning to write his memoirs, *Punch* alleged, under the title *Pencillings in the Palass; or, A Small Voice from the Royal Larder*!

For some reason or other, *Punch* wanted to make fun of the antiquary George Jones, author of the *History of Ancient America*. They tried to annoy him by claiming that he was the uncle of the Boy Jones, and by publishing various letters from the Boy to his 'uncle':

HMS *Warspite*, Gibraltar Roads
MY DEAR UNCLE – I am sorry to say that your book of *Ancient America*
that you gave me has been thrown overboard, by order of the Captain; its
weight was found so to stop the ship sailing. I thought, as I read it, that it got
heavier and heavier every day: and so it turned out; for it took ten men at last
to throw it overboard. If you write anything more, don't send it to me, for the
Captain swears 'twill waterlog the vessel.'

The reason the Boy Jones had fallen overboard, to be rescued by the lifebuoy,
had not been mischief-making, only that too much reading of *Ancient
America* had made him so sleepy he had fallen from the mast!

Another joke was that the Boy Jones took some part in the bombardment
of Tangiers, by a French fleet under the command of the Prince de Joinville.
An article on 'the Boy Jones and the Boy Joinville' boldly claimed that

> Jones is a genius. That of the millions who gaze upon the awful walls of
> Buckingham Palace, shut out from them as from Paradise, Jones should have
> been the only daring spirit that conceived a design to pass them – to dip his
> plebeian fingers in the custards of the royal larder – to creep up the royal
> chimneys – to crouch beneath the royal sofa, thereby (as his uncle, George
> Jones, has written to *Punch*,) 'causing her majesty so much alarm'. Surely, the
> merits of the Boy Joinville could not compare with his: 'let Joinville hover on
> the coast of Morocco, Britannia may be as mild as a Quakeress, for has she
> not at Gibraltar her babe of glory – the Jervis of the chimney – the Nelson
> of the larder – her Boy Jones'. A bright future awaited the Boy Jones: when
> Post-Captain Jones one day would kneel to receive his knighthood from the
> Queen, would she then recognise her old friend the 'Sweep in the Palace', and
> would George Jones still deny his brilliant nephew?

Edward Jones was to serve on board the *Warspite* for another full year.[7] It
was said that he was well behaved during this period of time, and a very
good seaman, considering the relatively short time he had been at sea. At
climbing he had no superior in the *Warspite*. On one occasion he climbed the
main truck (top of the tallest mast on the ship), seated himself there, tore off
his hat, jacket, and shirt, and flung them down to his shipmates on deck.[8] On
18 December 1845, Edward was transferred to the *Inconstant* and finally
promoted to ordinary seaman. During his year-long service on board this
vessel, there were no further attempts to escape; his conduct was marked as
'good', whereas on *Warspite* it had been 'fair' only.[9]

On 19 November 1846, the commander-in-chief of the Mediterranean fleet,
Vice-Admiral Sir William Parker, wrote a confidential letter to the First Lord
of the Admiralty, Lord Auckland, with a query what was to be done with

the Boy Jones.[10] After he had been dragged on board the *Warspite* for the second time back in October 1842, he had now served more than four years before the mast on various ships in the Mediterranean. When the *Inconstant* had been ordered back to England, Seaman Jones had been transferred to the *Siren*, since after the Portsmouth incident, there were orders that he was to be kept abroad, with as much distance as possible between him and Buckingham Palace. The problem was now that the *Siren* had since been ordered to the coast of Africa, where the climate was particularly unhealthy. Sir William Parker was thinking of transferring Jones to another ship, not from humanitarian feelings but because he feared that the death of the wretched state prisoner would cause 'unfortunate observations in the Newspapers'. Lord Auckland agreed that Jones should not be sent to Africa. He ought to be kept in the Mediterranean, where he could be closely watched on board ship, and where there was less risk he would die from disease. Enquiries should be made into his conduct, and if he was promising well, he should get an appointment at Malta Dockyards. Lord Auckland wrote to the former Lord Privy Seal, Lord Bessborough, who may well have been sworn into the original plot to get rid of the Boy Jones, to let him know about the outcome of his deliberations.

On 31 December 1846, Edward Jones was transferred from the *Inconstant* to the brig *Harlequin*. When this ship was off the coast of Syria in May 1847, it was visited by the Consul-General John Barker. He and his party had the opportunity, when grog was served, to see the notorious Boy Jones, who was once more shown as a curiosity. Not unnaturally for someone who had been pressed into service as a sailor and kept on board ship for more than five years against his will, a very sulky boy he looked.[11] There were still newspaper rumours about him back in England. In August 1847, the *Limerick Chronicle* and other newspapers reported that the notorious Boy Jones was serving as a trumpeter in the 8th Hussars, currently garrisoned in Limerick.[12] He was doing a good job, was 'perfectly cured of his wayward disposition', and one of the best men of the regiment. He was known to both officers and men only as 'the Boy Jones', and there were many jokes about his early exploits at Buckingham Palace. The Boy's old friends at the *Satirist* office in London pricked up their ears and exclaimed,

> Bravo! The boy Jones, he who crept so silently and secretly about Buckingham-house, and the royal palace, who evaded guards and royal flunkies, who set all London in an uproar, and every 'wonder-wounded hero' made to stand aghast, who amazed nursery-maids, and became the theme – the lion of every aristocratic gossip, is, it appears, determined to yet make a greater 'noise' in the world!

They could well remember when the Boy Jones 'was under the sofa on which her Majesty and Prince Al. sat. Think of the conversation he must have listened to (and what else we know not).' The Boy Jones was now sounding his own trumpet; would its fanfare soon again be heard from the depths of Buckingham Palace?[13] But after speaking to Henry Jones, a writer in the *Liverpool Mercury* could report that the Boy Jones was certainly not a trumpeter, but still serving on board the *Harlequin* now stationed at Smyrna.[14]

Absence makes the heart grow fonder, and Henry Jones and his wife kept longing for the return of their errant son, who had been taken away from them in such a dismal way. In October 1847, old Jones petitioned the Lords of the Admiralty that Edward should be allowed to come home. The Boy was now twenty-three years old, having served afloat for five and a half years. As could be expected from someone who has become a sailor against his will, his character had always been indifferent, and the plan to offer him an appointment at the Malta Dockyards was not acted upon. Moreover, both the Admiralty and the government officials must have been fearful that the Boy might die from accident or disease while serving afloat, and that the father would speak out in the newspapers to divulge that his son had been forced to serve in the Royal Navy without being either tried or convicted. With belated magnanimity, the Admiralty agreed that ordinary seaman Edward Jones was to be discharged from the *Harlequin* at Smyrna and given a free passage to London. Arriving in late January 1848, he moved in with his parents and siblings, who were still living in Bell-yard.[15] His old friends in the *Satirist* office were delighted the Boy Jones was back in London, warning the Queen that, although he had probably not yet made his mind up when to come and see her, he was one of those persons who turned up when least expected. During his years in the navy, he had gained favour by always *looking up* to his superiors, the punning went on, just like he had done when he lay underneath the sofa that supported Her Majesty's precious posterior.[16]

It would appear as if there was considerable sympathy for the returning Boy Jones among the poor people in Westminster and indignation that he had been pressed into becoming a sailor against his will. Whether this sympathy resulted in the Boy and his family receiving financial support is not known with certainty but would appear likely. According to a curious newspaper story from October 1848, one of the constables of the Mendicant Society encountered a feeble-looking beggar who hobbled along while bawling, 'I am the poor Boy Jones who was sent to sea for being found in the Palace. I am now discharged from the ship and have not the means of getting a crust of bread. Good Christians, give a helping hand and bestow a copper upon the unfortunate Boy Jones!' The mendicant constable recognised him as a notorious begging impostor, however, and although the 'sham Boy Jones' ran away with great alacrity, he was pursued, captured and imprisoned for a month with hard labour.[17]

What the real Boy Jones was doing at this time is not known, but there are serious fears that he was up to no good. There were several reports from the outskirts of London about a young man in the dress of a sailor entering houses and committing various petty thefts. On the morning of 24 August 1849, Police Sergeant William Welton was patrolling near Lewisham. He saw a young man carrying a large bundle of goods and stopped him, asking where he was going. 'To Greenwich,' the man answered sullenly. When asked where he came from, he again muttered 'Greenwich'. This made Sergeant Welton suspicious. He knew that, the evening before, the house of the Under-Sheriff of London, the wealthy solicitor Mr David Williams Wire, situated in Lewisham Road not far away, had been burgled. After gruffly demanding to see the contents of the man's bundle, the sailor unwillingly produced a timepiece, a black frock coat, a quantity of valuable plate, two towels, and a variety of other things. The young man, who identified himself as John Frost, a former sailor, was promptly taken into custody.[18]

When John Frost stood trial for burglary at the Old Bailey on 17 September, Sergeant Welton testified how he had captured the sailor Frost carrying the stolen goods, and Mr Wire's housekeeper could identify all the stolen goods as those belonging to her master. Although Frost objected that another man had given him these valuables to carry, he was convicted for burglary and sentenced to transportation for ten years. A few days later, when John Frost was still kept at Newgate awaiting transfer to the hulks, a police constable came to visit another prisoner. The moment he set eyes on 'Frost', he exclaimed, 'Hallo! How on earth did you come here, young Jones? You haven't been to see her Majesty again, have you?' It turned out that this constable had several times met and spoken to the Boy Jones when he had been in custody for entering Buckingham Palace. Although 'Frost' resolutely denied being the Boy Jones, he was positively recognised as the celebrated palace intruder by a number of other police constables and much laughed at as a result. With its usual flippancy, the *Satirist* questioned the wisdom of Jones changing his name to 'Frost' at the approach of the cold weather, since now his career seemed to have been 'nipped in the bud' in quite a serious manner. Another newspaper article claimed that the Boy Jones had been sent abroad to be honestly employed in an unnamed colony, but Jones had neatly eluded the powers that be:

> Do the palace chimneys require 'sweeping'; or are our Colonial authorities so loose in their duties, that the returned convict has been allowed to return to England *sub rosa*? Surely, this 'Boy Jones' will be a feature in the History of England![19]

But for someone proposed to become a feature of his country's history, the Boy Jones was not doing particularly well. At the age of just twenty-five, he was awaiting transportation to one of the dreaded antipodian prison colonies. It is likely that, during his long and dreary imprisonment at the hulks, he was still teased by both warders and prisoners, all of whom knew him as the notorious Boy Jones.

8

What Happened to the Boy Jones?

The *imp*udent urchin; whom, sure, the *Devil* owns,
And Government wants to send into the Navy,
Will not go to sea – and 'tis cunning of 'Jones',
Who thus may avoid his relation, 'Old Davy'!

Satirist, 21 March 1841

The prisoner John Frost, alias Edward Jones, remained on the hulks for the remainder of 1849, and for all of 1850, 1851, and 1852. After three and a half years on the hulks, he was finally transported to Western Australia on the *Pyrenees* convict ship on 31 January 1853.[1] After a long and perilous journey, the ship arrived at the Fremantle prison colony on 30 April. John Frost, alias Edward Jones, alias Convict No. 1861, correctly gave his date of birth as 1824, his occupation as a labourer, and his marital status as unmarried.[2] Under normal circumstances, he would have had to look forward to a lengthy period of hard labour and harsh treatment, before he would be allowed certain freedoms, or even a ticket of leave that allowed him to seek employment outside the prison.

But, surprisingly, the Fremantle prison records show that the convict Frost was granted a ticket of leave on 1 May, the day after he had arrived. It would seem as if, during his lengthy incarceration on the hulks, some influential person had made a 'deal' with the Boy: as long as he stayed in Fremantle, far away from Buckingham Palace, he would not be mistreated or suffer enforced hard labour. It seems as if a job had been found for the Boy Jones, as assistant to a maker of pies. At least, a gentleman who visited Fremantle some time in the mid-1850s had a pie-seller pointed out to him as 'the "Boy Jones", the individual whose anxiety for an interview with Her Majesty led him to present himself through the unusual medium of the chimney ...' He could hardly believe that this scruffy-looking Australian retailer of 'Hot pies, Pies all hot' was the great celebrity of 1841.[3]

The alias 'Frost' soon wore off, and Edward Jones became notorious once more. He was known only as 'the Boy Jones' among the inhabitants of Fremantle. Lieutenant Edmund Du Cane, the supervisor of convict labour in Western Australia, later wrote an article about his experiences, in which he stressed that the Fremantle convicts and ticket-of-leave men were law-abiding characters, who did not try to escape. He himself had lived very near the prisoners' depot, but had never suffered theft or assault. In fact, 'the only case that ever occurred of trespass in my grounds, at unlawful seasons, was when once the celebrated "boy Jones" (whose lofty aspirations toward high life had not met with success) broke out of the depot about ten o'clock *to complain that the lights had been put out too early!*'[4]

But, as we know, the Boy Jones was not the kind of person to remain in one place for very long if he could avoid it. Maybe his dreary job selling pies became too much to bear; perhaps he was still being annoyed by people who wanted to see him as a curiosity; or just possibly the lure of Buckingham Palace became too much for him. At any rate, he seems to have found some means to return to England in late 1855 or early 1856.

On the evening of Saturday 10 May 1856, Major-General George Morton Eden, the commander-in-chief of the western army district, had been sitting in his Plymouth study reading some important and secret army documents. The morning after, he was aghast to find that these documents had been strewn about, like if some intruder had looked through them. Fearing that a spy or burglar had ransacked his study, the General had a look round his house, but he found that the only thing missing was a gold sash from one of his dress uniforms. When he went out to question the sentries who had been stationed nearby, one of them said that, during the night in question, he had seen a scruffy-looking character dressed like a sailor lurking about. According to his instructions, he had challenged this individual and taken him in charge. When the 'sailor' had told him he was just looking for somewhere to sleep, the sentry had driven him away. Later during his rounds, the sentry had seen that the door to the General's garden had been left open.

General Eden reported the theft to Superintendent Robert Hutchman of the Devonport Police. This experienced police officer soon made several important breakthroughs. It turned out that, on 11 May, an unknown sailor had been drinking at the Red Lion public house. When this sottish fellow had run out of money, he gave a gold sash to the beer-house keeper John Stantiford to purchase more ale. He gave his name as John Jones and boasted that he had taken the sash home from the Crimean war, where he had been serving on board HMS *Harlequin*. But having read about the theft in the newspaper, the publican gave the sash to the police, along with a description of the sailor Jones. The Devonport police constables tracked Jones down on 13 May and took him into custody. The sailor told them that, a few days earlier, he had got very drunk and fallen in with two men whose names he did not know, one of whom had given him the gold sash in security for a loan of 10 shillings, but this story was not believed.[5]

When Jones was put on trial at the Devonport Midsummer Quarter Sessions, indicted with stealing the gold sash from General Eden's house, both sentry and beer-house keeper identified him as the sailor they had seen. The recorder sentenced him to six months hard labour, reminding Jones that he was very fortunate this was a case of simple larceny and not burglary. It was suspected that Jones had for some time been roaming the countryside in the guise of a seaman's dress, at times entering houses and gardens to steal what opportunity offered. A few days later, the true identity of the thief was discovered. *The Times* and several other newspapers reported that the Boy Jones of Buckingham Palace notoriety was now undergoing punishment in Devonport Gaol for stealing from the house of Major-General Eden.[6]

Amused that their old friend the Boy had resurfaced once more, *Punch* recalled the earlier story about him trying to escape in Athens, and allegedly entering the Royal Palace. Since King Otho might soon be forced to abdicate, should the Boy Jones not be appointed his successor?

> Jones the First would at least be as majestic, would at least make as respectable a father of the Greek people as the first Otho, whose better part of Royalty is that better half, his wife. All the instincts of Jones smack of Royalty. Is it not his boast that, adventuring into the nursery of English Royalty, it was his high privilege to hear a Royal baby cry? Our voice is – 'Vive Jones the First, King of Greece!' His elevation may be quietly managed, and at almost no expense; the only necessary cost will be for the enlargement of the crown; for what suits the pippin of Otho can hardly fit 'that globe of thought, that palace of the soul', surmounting the shoulders of Jones.[7]

The unexpected return of the Boy Jones also inspired a chapter in Sir Arthur Hallam Elton's *Tracts for the Present Crisis*. In-I-Go Jones had been imprisoned and safely stowed away in one of her Majesty's ships of war in the hope it would teach him better manners, he wrote. But in Elton's facetious account, he was back to spy on royalty, although 'we thought he was disposed of, personal attire sold for a low figure to Madame Tussaud, and a cast of his skull, with the bump of curiosity and self-esteem largely developed, put in the Phrenological Museum.'

After he had been released from prison in 1857, there are fewer sources about the Boy Jones. The fact that, back in 1848, he had been transported under the name 'John Frost' seems to have saved him from being prosecuted for the very serious crime of returning from transportation. His family were still living in London: his octogenarian father, his fifty-year-old mother, his blind sister Elizabeth and his younger twin sisters Mary and Julia.[8] Mary seems to have been a somewhat loose character who was once prosecuted for stealing from two old women who kept a mangle and who narrowly escaped being transported in 1854 for stealing 4 sovereigns from her master.[9] The 1861 census has the Jones family living in York-street not far from Bell-yard, but Edward's name is not among them. Instead, it would appear as if his younger brother, who had become a respectable civil servant in Australia, helped the Boy financially and encouraged him to avoid further burglarious activities. Perhaps this brother got in touch with representatives of the government who were still keen to get rid of the Boy, to prevent further 'visits' to Buckingham Palace. They may have made a plan to help the Boy emigrate to Australia, where it would be easier for him to earn an honest living. Once he was gone, the Queen would be safe from her stalker.

In September 1868, a newspaper could report that Mr Jones, who had just been made Minister of Public Works in Victoria, was in fact the brother of the notorious Boy. Both had started life at the very bottom of society, and the advancement of Mr Jones was heralded as 'a singular illustration of the changes that take place in new and thriving colonies'. The Boy Jones was also in Australia, the journalist claimed, and a few years earlier, he had been leading an industrious life and living with his brother in Melbourne.[10] In 1871, a punning journalist could report that Boy Jones, the famous chimney sweep, had died in London. He had been sent to Australia 'after various other modes of correcting his eccentricities had been tried in vain', but returned from Sydney two years earlier. His death was caused by his pure, true love for the Queen, the journalist went on. Some unfeeling person had abruptly told him that Queen Victoria was dead, and instantly Jones fell down and died too; in fact, 'Jones made a clean sweep of himself!'[11] This article was clearly written as a feeble attempt at a joke, but it does support the notion that Jones had resided in Australia for some time. According to a gossipy old book about Queen Victoria's early days on the throne, the Boy Jones, whose singular 'Palace-breaking mania' had made him such a celebrity, 'was finally induced to go to Australia, where, it is said, he grew up to be a well-to-do colonist.'[12]

In his memoirs, journalist Sir Henry Lucy mentions that, in 1899, he wrote a magazine article asking 'what had become of "the Boy Jones" who more than once in the first year of the Queen's married life made his way into Buckingham Palace, and was hauled forth from beneath sofas and four-posters'. Had he lived and prospered, to become the Man Jones, or perhaps even the Grandfather Jones? A resident of Perth, West Australia, wrote back to him with some extraordinary information, namely that the Boy Jones had emigrated to Perth, where he 'rose to the high estate of town crier!' Unfortunately, the Boy Jones's fame had preceded him:

When he went forth, bell in hand, to perform his important functions, the naughty boys of Perth were accustomed to gather round him and make pointed inquiries as to the approaches to Buckingham Palace, the health of the Queen, and the appearance of the baby who is today Dowager Empress of Germany. The man Jones, angered beyond self-restraint, occasionally made dashes at the enemy, committing assaults which made his appearance in the police court familiar. He died about four years ago.[13]

So, what happened to the Boy Jones in the end? By remarkable coincidence, I was able to find out. In 2002, the ABC TV series *Victoria and Albert* was transmitted in Australia. This TV series featured a poor unfortunate chimney sweep trying to break into Windsor Castle, but being caught and harshly spoken to by Prince Albert. In spite of the lack of knowledge of Boy Jones lore displayed by the Australian TV writers, Mr Tim Gibson, of Bairnsdale in Victoria, thought he had heard this story before. He wrote a letter to the *Age* newspaper claiming that not only had the incident really happened, and sparked a furore over lax security at the royal residences, but the Boy had been living in Australia for some considerable period of time, before ending up in an unmarked grave in Bairnsdale cemetery.[14]

Through contacting the East Gippsland Historical Society, I was able to find out the details. On Boxing Day 1893, an old man known locally as Thomas Jones had decided to go into Bairnsdale to get something to drink. He was lodging with a fireman named George John Hadfield, who lived on the Sarsfield road three and a half miles from Bairnsdale. Although the fireman knew that Jones often drank to excess, and that he was seldom sober when returning from his expeditions to Bairnsdale, he gave the old man a Christmas present of 10 shillings. Thomas Jones trudged into Bairnsdale, bought some spirits, and lay down on the wing of the Mitchell River bridge swigging from his bottle. Although several people saw the old man lying there, none of them saw fit to warn him that this was quite a dangerous position for a drunken person. Later the same afternoon, the semi-stuporous Jones rolled over the edge of the parapet and fell twelve feet, striking his head hard against a large stone and expiring shortly after.

At the inquest, the fireman Hadfield deposed that he had known Jones for five or six years and that he had provided him with a home. Jones had said that he was around seventy-three years old and unmarried, with no living relatives in this part of Australia. It was concluded that the inebriated old man had accidentally fallen off the bridge and died from the head injuries caused by his impact on the stone. A few days later, the *Bairnsdale Advertiser* had a startling story to tell. In his less reticent moods, Jones had told his drinking companions some spicy stories about his early life in England. Once upon a time, he had been apprenticed to the sweep who had the contract for sweeping the chimneys at Windsor Castle. By crawling up and down the chimneys, he soon acquired a working knowledge of the rooms of the castle. On the occasion of the marriage of Queen Victoria and Prince Albert, the mischievous lad had decided to pay them a visit. He climbed down the chimney of the Queen's bedroom and hid underneath the bed. But before the arrival of the newly wedded couple, he was discovered and ignominiously dragged forth. He was transported to the penal settlement in Tasmania before gaining his freedom and going to Australia, where he had been living for many years. Although, when sober, Jones had been quite sensitive to any allusion to this sensational episode of his youth, and resented any person questioning him about his royal connections, several old acquaintances of his vouched for the story being nothing but the truth.[15]

The question is, of course, how much this rather facetious account, in an obscure Australian newspaper, can be relied upon. It should be noted, however, that the year 1895 exactly coincides with the year of the Boy Jones's demise given by Sir Henry Lucy's Australian correspondent. The Boy Jones had changed his name before, and it would have made sense for him to have done so once again, due to his unwanted notoriety in Perth and elsewhere. And for a drunken Australian, there was little to differ Buckingham Palace from Windsor Castle.

Thus it would seem as if the man who had once been the celebrated Boy Jones ended his days in ignominy: a sad, lonely, drunken old man living in an obscure part of Australia. There are three alternative endings to the story, all of them unfortunately quite untrue. Answering a query from a correspondent, the *London Journal* of October 1866 alleged that the Boy Jones 'was sent on board a man of war, as a naval apprentice', but near the Cape of Good Hope, he fell into the sea from the yardarm and was drowned.[16] But as we know, there is evidence from multiple trustworthy sources that the Boy Jones came through his naval career unscathed and stepped ashore for good in 1848, ending his six years as an involuntary seaman. In 1897, an article in the *Tit-Bits* magazine found it probable that, after his adventures as an involuntary sailor, the Boy Jones had been consigned to an asylum.[17] Again, as we know, this cannot have been the case, since his movements from 1848 until 1857 can be traced in some detail.

The New York Times came up with an even taller story in 1910.[18] A feature writer for this newspaper, identified only as 'a Veteran Diplomat', entertained the readers with various yarns about criminal lunatics. Among his startling claims was that 'that extraordinary "Boy Jones" (when I met him an elderly and respectable looking man)' had been detained in Broadmoor. This meeting was supposed to have happened in the early days of this institution, when a 'Dr Meyers' was 'director'. But Broadmoor was built in 1863 and its first Physician Superintendent, Dr John Meyer, died in 1870, when Edward Jones was just forty-six years old and hardly an elderly man. There is no Edward Jones listed in the Broadmoor admissions registers from 1863 until 1900, nor any other individual named Jones born in or around 1824.[19] The *New York Times* article contains numerous errors, one of them the assertion that Jack the Ripper himself ended up in Broadmoor, and is likely to be a rehash of old news about notable criminals and lunatics, with some tall stories added to the mix to generate interest among the American newspaper readers.

9

The Boy Jones in Literature & Drama

A fact, the 'Boy Jones' who, in our days, with malice
Aforethought, so often got into the Palace,
Would seem to confirm, as, 'tis whispered he owns, he's
The son of a natural son of Tom Jones's!

Richard Harris Barham, 'The Wedding Day', from *The Ingoldsby Legends*

One of the most popular novelists of the 1840s and 1850s was George William MacArthur Reynolds. In his time, his novels outsold those of Dickens and Thackeray, although they have not enjoyed the same durability. Reynolds had been born in 1814, the son of a distinguished naval officer. He inherited a good deal of money as a young man but spent it all on a harebrained scheme to start a newspaper in Paris. After returning to London bankrupt in 1836, he had to support himself with all forms of literary hackwork, including plagiarising the early works of Charles Dickens. Not unnaturally, Dickens took exception to seeing his characters rendered into buffoons in Reynolds's *Pickwick Abroad* and *Pickwick Married*, and later in *Master Timothy's Bookcase*, a knock-off of *Master Humphrey's Clock*. His opinion of Reynolds would always remain very low.

Having experienced some degree of poverty himself, G. W. M. Reynolds became a political radical. He resented Dickens, whom he considered to be posing as a man of the people, although he fawned to the rich and famous and accumulated much money and renown from his dismal, overrated books. Reynolds felt that his own work did much more than Dickens's insipid stories to reflect the plight of London's urban poor. After being inspired by Eugene Sue's *Les Mystères de Paris*, an epic melodrama of the Parisian slums, he began writing *The Mysteries of London*, a long and rambling novel that he hoped would change his failing fortunes.

In the centre of the labyrinthine plot of the *Mysteries* are two brothers, Eugene and Richard Markham: one a vicious libertine, the other a forthright, honourable and heroic character. Eugene slithers through the novel's myriad of pages like a venomous reptile, leaving seduced women, cheated businessmen and betrayed political opponents in his wake. Richard comes across as a Victorian superhero, fighting sinister villains like the cadaverous, grave-robbing Resurrection Man and his burglarious sidekick, the Cracksman.

In Chapter LVII of *The Mysteries of London*, a new character is introduced, the young pot-boy Henry Holford. He is described as aged about sixteen or seventeen but looking even younger, very short in stature and with effeminate good looks. Holford has been bribed by the Resurrection Man and the Cracksman to act as a 'scout' for one of their burglaries: amazingly, the two villains aim to break into Buckingham Palace itself. On New Year's Day 1839, the two villains hoist the young lad over the wall of the Palace Gardens on Constitution Hill, and Holford successfully enters the palace. Hiding underneath a sofa in the Sculpture Gallery, he feasts his eyes on the lords, ladies and politicians attending a sumptuous evening party. Queen Victoria herself is his favourite. Enthralled, Holford admires her elegant clothes, pretty face and 'magnificent bosom'. After the party has ended and the royal domestics have extinguished the lights and withdrawn, Holford sits on the very sofa formerly occupied by his beloved Queen. He bemoans his lowly position in life: although seated on the very sofa that had formerly hugged the backsides of royalty, he still remains the miserable young Henry Holford, the pot-boy and amateur burglar. Holford's encounter with Queen Victoria has entirely put him off helping to burgle the house of his idol. Instead, he follows the example of the Boy Jones and tucks in at the unprotected royal larder, before falling asleep underneath his favourite sofa, hoping to see his beloved Queen again the next day.

Early the following morning, Holford goes for a stroll around the palace. He visits the Picture Gallery, the Dining Room and the Throne Room, where he removes the cover and sits on the throne. He goes to the kitchen to fetch some delicious food, before returning to eavesdrop on two noble ladies. They gossip about Queen Victoria's forthcoming marriage to Prince Albert, dropping dark hints about the insanity running in the royal family, and the rumours of George III's secret marriage to the Quaker girl Hannah Lightfoot, which, if true, would render the entire royal family illegitimate. Later, Queen Victoria and Prince Albert have a private tête-à-tête seated on the very sofa under which Holford is hiding. The lewd-minded Reynolds is uncharacteristically reticent when retelling what Holford observed:

> We shall not record any portion of their discourse – animated, interesting, and tender though it were; suffice it to say, that for a short time they seemed to forget their high rank, and to throw aside the trammels of court etiquette, in order to give vent to their natural feelings which the sovereign has in common with the peasant.

Early the next morning, when Holford goes to the royal larder to have a meal, he is startled by another individual nearby. It is not one of the bumbling royal servants, but the sinister, cadaverous Resurrection Man, who has come to look for his apprentice burglar. Holford manages to convince him that, since the Queen will leave Buckingham Palace for Windsor Castle in a few days, there would be risk-free ample pickings for the burglars at this latter date. Although neither burglar had met with any impediment during their stay in the Queen's palace, the Resurrection Man agrees to withdraw. But when they join forces with the Cracksman at the Boozing-Ken, a nearby hostelry for thieves and vagabonds, the Resurrection Man shows a more sinister side of his character. He suspects that Holford is cheating them and invites him to another drinking-den, the Dark House in Brick-lane, Spitalfields. Here, the two villains plan to drug Holford's beer and lock him up in a secret dungeon until he confesses. But showing unexpected good sense, Holford instead seeks out the dashing Richard Markham, who leads a police raid on the Dark House. The Resurrection Man and the Cracksman escape, however, after firing off a powerful bomb that reduces the alehouse to rubble.

One would have expected that this narrow escape from being murdered would have kept Henry Holford away from further criminal capers, but this is far from the case. Infatuated with the Queen and jealous of Prince Albert, the adventurous pot-boy pays multiple visits to Buckingham Palace, to spy on the royal couple and listen to the court gossip. Once, he hides underneath a sofa to eavesdrop on the Queen and Prince having breakfast together. It turns out that the haughty, isolated royals are completely out of touch with the lives of ordinary people, reading newspaper reports of destitute and suicidal people without comprehending them in the slightest. But after the Queen has withdrawn, Prince Albert sees Holford lurking underneath the sofa and exclaims, 'Come forth, whoever you may be!'

The miserable pot-boy cravenly begs for mercy, assuring that his intrusion was only caused by his 'invincible curiosity' about court life. The magnanimous Prince does not punish him, but merely expels him from Buckingham Palace.

Henry Holford is deeply humiliated, since he feels that his 'rival' Prince Albert has expelled him from his paradisiacal existence in Buckingham Palace, close to his beloved Queen. He starts reading books about royal assassins, exclaiming that it would be glorious to be ranked with 'those gallant few who have either slain, or attempted the lives of monarchs or great men!' The demented pot-boy borrows a brace of pistols from his friend, the returned convict Crankey Jem, goes to Constitution Hill, and waits there for the Queen and Prince to come past in their carriage. He fires one of his 'barkers' at them but misses; just as he is to discharge the second one, he is grabbed behind by Crankey Jem, who had followed him clandestinely. Holford is arrested, examined at the Home Office, and confined to Bedlam indefinitely. Belatedly, he regrets his morbid ambition to become a royal assassin, since it has landed him in this dreadful madhouse. Although entirely sane, he is immured into a living tomb, surrounded by lunatics who had committed the most appalling crimes.

Henry Holford is clearly a composite of two characters. Firstly, his obsession with the Queen and mania for entering Buckingham Palace closely mirror those of the Boy Jones. Making his own interpretation of the secretive Boy's motivation to seek out Queen Victoria again and again, Reynolds presumes that Holford falls in love with the young Queen. Like the majority of the male characters in *The Mysteries of London*, Holford has little time for platonic admiration from afar: he is driven by an earthy sexual desire for the Queen, sighing over her buxom body and magnificent bust. Secondly, Holford's occupation as a pot-boy, his unsuccessful attempt to assassinate the Queen, and his incarceration in Bedlam are all features from the sad story of Edward Oxford.[1]

According to Charles Hindley, the biographer of James Catnach, 'It's that Boy Jones again' was a popular byword in the 1840s, made use of when anything was unexpectedly missing in the household.[2] According to several dictionaries of Victorian slang, a 'Boy Jones' was a virtual catchphrase for a teller of secrets, or an unnamed informant.[3] For quite some time, 'Boy Jones' was also a byword for any sneaky character who wished to enter houses to spy on their rightful inhabitants, either as a 'Peeping Tom' or with blackmail in mind. The expression occurs in as lofty a literary work as James Joyce's *Ulysses*, where Chapter 16 contains a reference to 'some anonymous letter from the usual boy Jones, who happened to come across them at the crucial moment in a loving position locked in one another's arms ...'.

The impact on the Boy Jones on Victorian culture can be judged from the following quotation from a magazine article written in 1855, quite a few years after the Boy Jones hysteria in 1841:

'The Boy Jones': what an absolutely fame that individual has realized: not limited by England or by Europe, but a household word in America, India, Australia. *Cui non notus Hylas puer?* Who has not heard of the Boy Jones, wherever the English language is spoken? Name for name, the Boy Jones reaches many times further than Lord Raglan. And yet was there ever an individual more obscure, or more meriting obscurity, than this unadmirable personage?[4]

Throughout the nineteenth century, the Boy Jones and his exploits were used as metaphors by many authors, from learned scholars to punning journalists, in a variety of high- and low-brow publications. In 1842, a satirical Irish writer compared the social-climbing American poet N. P. Willis, author of

Letters from Under a Bridge, to the Boy Jones:

> Willis has a craving appetite for court gossip, and the tittle-tattle of a palace: so had the boy Jones. Willis established himself as a listener in society: so did the boy Jones. Willis obtruded himself into places, and among people where he had no possible pretention to be seen: so did the boy Jones. Willis wrote letters from under a bridge: the boy Jones ate mutton chops under a sofa.[5]

In 1848, a reviewer of Forster's *Life of Goldsmith* discussed the phenomenon of celebrities having patronage to publish books with the words

> for instance, had the boy Jones (otherwise called Inigo Jones) possessed enough of book-making skill to forge a plausible curtain-lecture, as overheard by himself when concealed in her Majesty's bed-room, ten steam-presses working day and night would not have supplied the public demand; and even her majesty must herself have sent for a large-paper copy ...[6]

In a sporting magazine, an authority on greyhound racing recommended that 'the dog bill be pushed into Parliament with as much determination as the Boy Jones pushed himself into the Palace'. Another author in the same magazine exclaimed that every person 'peer or peasant, from Sardanapalus to the Boy Jones' should find attraction in a sporting life.[7]

An antiquary found it hilarious that when the eccentricities of the Boy Jones on dry land had been put an end to, he jumped into the sea so that he could enjoy the luxury of being saved from drowning.[8] An opera critic presumed that the *raptures* of the lovesick Boy Jones had led him to be *transported* in quite different fashion.[9] The writer of an article on notable criminals wrongly supposed that

> the 'boy Jones' who figures so largely in the police reports some years ago for having forced his way into Buckingham palace in order to discover the secrets of royalty, was as much a notable among his comrades as any of the *gamins de Paris* mentioned by Victor Hugo.[10]

Author George Augustus Sala declared that he was 'not the Boy Jones, to hide under the sofa, and listen to the conversation of my sovereign'. In an article on his travels in Russia, he asked the reader to 'imagine a wedding trousseau, all daintily displayed – all satin, gauze, orange flowers, Brussels lace, and pink rosettes – which had been clumsily handled by some Boy Jones? Imagine the marks of thumbs and greasy, sooty fingers dimly disfiguring the rich textures? That to me, is Russian civilisation.'[11]

It also seems as if every male person named Jones was at risk of being nicknamed 'the Boy' at this time. In his memoirs, jurist and historian

Frederic Harrison remembered he and his youthful companions 'chuckled over the gymnastics of the "Boy Jones" who climbed over the wall and down the chimney at Buckingham Palace in order to "see the Queen at Home". As we could see the Queen any day driving or riding, we wanted to have him flogged before he was transported. I had a school-fellow with the name of Jones and he never lost the nickname I gave him – "the Boy Jones".'[12] Australian cricketer S. R. Jones, a useful opening batsman in the 1880s, shared the same fate.[13] Poet and politician Richard Monckton Milner, later Lord Houghton, was called 'In-I-Go Jones', 'in allusion to the feats of the "Boy Jones" in insinuating himself into Buckingham Palace', possibly because of his social climbing tendencies.[14] When asked by the Duke of Devonshire to provide some imaginary titles for books, the celebrated poet Thomas Hood came up with 'In-I-Go on Secret Entrances'.[15]

It would take until 1943 for another full-length fictional representation of the Boy Jones and his extraordinary career. Patricia Gordon, an American writer of children's books, published *The Boy Jones*, a fanciful work that presents life in Victorian London in a way that would make both Charles Dickens and G. W. R. Reynolds cringe.[16] People are uniformly kind and benign, and although he is said to be poor, the cheerful young Boy Jones can attend a good school and amuse himself with various pranks. He delivers a cake to Lady Sandwich who becomes his 'fairy godmother' and gives him half a crown to finance a grand birthday party. For reasons left unstated, the Boy develops a fixed idea to enter Buckingham Palace. On his first visit, he enters the kitchen, where he is given milk and bread by one of the maids. He wanders about at random, spies on the Queen for a while, and then leaves unimpeded. On his second visit, he again strolls about at will, and sits on the throne, but is later dragged out from under a sofa by an angry under-butler. He is sentenced to four months in prison, where he is treated very well, with Lady Sandwich sending hampers of food. When set at liberty, he tries his luck at the palace once more, but is arrested by Prince Albert in person and sent back to prison for four more months. After a fourth visit, he is again captured and sent to sea on the *Warspite*, where he is befriended by the kind and generous officers and sailors. In the Mediterranean, he jumps overboard one day and is lost and presumed dead. But not long after, a footman is employed at Buckingham Palace under the name of *Johnson*, at Lady Sandwich's personal recommendation. Thus all ends well for the inquisitive Boy, since in his new job he can do nothing else all day but gaze at the glories of royalty.

The Gordon book was closely followed by another weird spin on the Boy Jones tale, this time by the American journalist Theodore Bonnet. In his 1949 novel *The Mudlark*, a young street urchin, known as the Boy Wheeler, makes a precarious living by scavenging and selling what he could find on the muddy banks of the Thames.[17] The year is 1875. One day, he finds a locket containing a portrait of an elderly Queen Victoria; not knowing who she is, a colleague explains to him that she is the Mother of all England. Wanting to see the Queen, the Mudlark sneaks into Windsor Castle. He is discovered hiding just a few feet from Queen Victoria's chair but successfully evades capture. Later on, he is apprehended by the palace guards when he is sitting on the throne. He is suspected to have taken part in an assassination plot against the Queen. According to a newspaper, 'The guilty wretch is described as being of deformed body, swarthy complexion and a most forbidding mien.' But the kindly Prime Minister, Benjamin Disraeli, recognises that the Boy Wheeler is innocent and pleads for him in Parliament. Having been a recluse for a long time, mourning her beloved Prince Albert, the Queen is so moved upon meeting her juvenile admirer for the first time that she again enters public life, just in time for her Diamond Jubilee. As for the Boy Wheeler, he is offered a contract at a London music hall, but goes to school instead. He reappears in 1880 as a cabin boy on board the barque *Elizabeth P. Summers*, from which ship he wantonly jumps into the sea for the pleasure of seeing the lifebuoy light burning.

From this brief summary of the plot, Bonnet's book may sound quite amusing, but a modern reader forced to plough through all its 305 pages would be unlikely to agree. The book is quite boring, with dull characters and plentiful *longueurs*. As an American, Bonnet had to use his imagination to capture the Boy's Cockney dialect, and the results are quite ludicrous. John Brown's Scotch brogue is of a similar quality. But still, this sentimental rehash of the Boy Jones story received a major boost when it was made into a major film by Twentieth Century Fox, starring Irene Dunne as Queen Victoria and Alec Guinness as Disraeli. Since this lavish costume drama drew considerable cinema audiences on both sides of the Atlantic, the talented child actor Andrew Ray became an overnight star as the Mudlark. On the American film posters, he was portrayed in shabby Victorian attire, with the text 'At last it's here! The story of the Kid who wanted to sit on the Queen's throne!'

For the next dramatisation of the Boy Jones story we are indebted to the Canadian author and playwright Sky Gilbert. Described in an article as 'a novelist, theatre director and drag queen extraordinaire', Gilbert had for many years been entertaining his countrymen with various avant-garde plays. For reasons unknown, he one day chanced upon the Boy Jones story, and it was not long before his play with the same title premiered at the University of Toronto Drama Centre in early 2002. Although the main protagonist is called Edwin rather than Edward Jones, there is evidence that Gilbert had studied the story quite carefully, since he gets the names and activities of the supporting cast quite right.[18] A playwright rather than a historian, he takes major liberties with his storyline, however, particularly when he makes not only the Boy Jones himself but also several other characters into homosexuals.

The tobacconist Elgar was the Boy's 'nearest and dearest friend', kissing and fondling him on stage. The homophobic Mr James, who is as obnoxious as a stage villain as he was in real life, was sure that Elgar was his 'queerest friend' as well. The play is quite witty and amusing, with several musical interludes. One of these, 'The Undies of the Queen are Beautiful' was sung by the Boy himself, after he had been hired by an impresario to perform in a rowdy London tavern. Holding up some of the Queen's underwear he has stolen at Buckingham Palace, he warbles away:

Oi been to see the palace of the Queen
To me it did not seem to be so fine.
The houses parliament, they aren't worth a bloody cent,
And the chiming of Big Ben, Oi could miss that once again.
But one thing Oi'd visit every day,
The one thing Oi'd give a week of pay,
Cause Oi love 'em most of all, tho' they're something very small,
Oh, the bleeding blooming truth is that Oi love them more than you!
The Undies of the Queen are Beautiful
They speak in volumes yet they say but naught
For the truth it can be said, is not always in her 'ead
Oh, the Undies of the Queen are Beautiful!

The dismal Mr James, who is present to heckle the Boy, screams 'Sacrilege!' and throws a crusty bun at the palace intruder, scoring a direct hit.

The Boy's musical career was ended after he entered Buckingham Palace once more. When eavesdropping on the Queen and Prince, he was amazed that the conversation of these god-like personages was quite banal: the Prince complained that his feet felt sore from too much dancing. But the 'bad guys' take the Boy into custody and kidnap him on board the *Warspite*. The lovestruck Elgar comes too late to rescue him, and is left behind on the quay, to sing:

Oh how I miss that boy, that brilliant, foolish boy,
Will he ever survive the sea!

In the final scene, Queen Victoria and Prince Albert are chatting in their parlour on one half of the stage, while the Boy Jones is scrubbing the deck of the *Warspite* on the other. When the Boy looks for a lighted buoy, the Queen thinks she can see a light as well and walks over to a window; for a brief moment, they seem to be looking straight at each other. The reviews of Sky Gilbert's *The Boy Jones* were not particularly good: the prudish Canadian theatrical critics were annoyed by its indecent jokes, bawdy songs and hints of paedophilia. It would probably have done much better in London or New York.[19]

The most recent take on the Boy Jones story is the musical *Jones*, written by Bob Forrest-Webb with music by Peter Gritton and performed in late 2006 by the boys of Colet Court, the preparatory school to the fashionable St Paul's School in Barnes, West London. The Boy is now called Edmund Jones and his adventures have also been spiced up: far from being a thieving palace intruder, he is a pure-hearted chimney sweep's boy who manages to hide from Flume, the cruel master of the chimney sweeps at Buckingham Palace. Lurking in the palace chimneys, he befriends Queen Victoria's children, who help him attempt to escape. In the end, he turns out to be a hero, foiling a plot to assassinate the Queen. *Jones* the musical had its world premiere in November 2006 and performed to a packed house each night. Its youthful cast is said to have acquitted themselves very well, and the music attracted particular praise from the reviewers. The authors have informed me that they are in the process of making the musical into a film, along the lines of the celebrated *Oliver*.

10

Uninvited Visitors to Royalty

'In-I-go!' Jones said, as up the sash he threw,
'Out I come again', quoth he, and to the pantry flew.

From the *Satirist* of 4 April 1841

After the Boy Jones had been disposed of and the hysteria around him had finally died down, calm was restored to Buckingham Palace and its inhabitants. This calm would last for the better part of a century. Palace security, which had already been upgraded as a result of the Boy Jones incidents, received a further boost in 1842 and 1843 when Prince Albert and his new advisor Baron Stockmar undertook a reorganisation of the royal household.[1] They terminated the old 'grace and favour' system that had been so detrimental to the efficiency of the royal household and paved the way for the intrusions of the Boy Jones. Prince Albert and Baron Stockmar made all palace staff accountable to the Master of the Royal Household and abolished various archaic offices and inert functionaries. Importantly, they also reinforced court etiquette and made royalty less approachable.

By 1842, there had been not less than three attempts to assassinate the Queen, by Oxford, Francis and Bean. Although none of these incompetent, young would-be regicides had even come close to hitting their target, it was no longer possible for the Queen to travel about London in an open landau, with just a few pages in attendance. Considering the three assassination attempts, and the Boy Jones's multiple intrusions, it was clear to Prince Albert and Baron Stockmar that further expenditure on palace security was money well spent. Firstly, they made sure that a complement of army sentries guarded all entrances. Secondly, a strong party of police from the 'A' Division were to be patrolling the interior of the palace both day and night, and at the tradesman's entrance, there would always be a policeman in plain clothes. Thirdly, the royal livery porters were reorganised, with young, vigorous porters being recruited to replace some of their elderly colleagues. Another improvement was that, when the livery porters went off duty at 10 p.m., a party of night porters relieved them at the various porter's lodges and stations and stayed throughout the night. These belated reforms would appear to have had the desired effect. Madmen and tramps straying into the palace grounds were promptly arrested, and for the remainder of her long reign, Queen Victoria would remain safe from palace intruders.

It would in fact take more than three quarters of a century for any Boy Jones copycat to try to emulate his exploits. In the early morning of 7 June 1914, the motor fitter's mate George Pike was lurching home through the Pimlico streets after having visited a number of public houses.[2] Having read about the suffragettes trying to enter the grounds of Buckingham Palace, he decided to have a go himself when he saw the palace wall with its spiked railings. After successfully scaling the wall, he sneaked up to the palace and tried several windows, before finding an open basement door and entering the sleeping quarters of the royal servants. Through trial and error, he opened various doors, making polite excuses each time he woke someone up, but finally finding an empty room where he could steal an elegant suit of clothes. Looking the perfect gentleman, Pike took an early morning stroll round the palace, looking into various bedrooms. At one stage, he was not far away from the sleeping quarters of Queen Mary. But when Pike was challenged by a suspicious page, he lost his cool and ran, only to be tackled and arrested by his pyjama-clad adversary.

When he was brought up at Bow Street police court a few days later, Pike claimed that he had been drunk and that it had all been a mad freak, done out of bravado. A very short, timid-looking man, he certainly looked nothing like a conniving royal assassin. He did not have a criminal record and his employer gave him high marks for industry and reliability, with the caveat that 'he had been on the drink for some considerable time'. When Pike's old mother, who was very deaf, went into the box to speak for her son, she added a touch of pathos to the proceedings by exclaiming 'He has been a good son ever since he was born!' in a stentorian voice when asked to explain his extraordinary conduct. The magistrate spoke harshly to Pike, and it looked like he would receive a custodial sentence for his prank, but the magnanimous King George V interceded on his behalf. Pike was released on 15 June, giving a bond that he would be of good behaviour in the future.

Buckingham Palace chronicler Bruce Graeme wrote that the police had initially feared that Pike was a suffragette sympathiser, since they knew that the redoubtable Mrs Pankhurst and her friends had boasted that they would gain access to the palace by fair means or foul. It turned out that he was not connected with 'these militant and undignified ladies', as Graeme expressed it, but 'an independent intruder, probably desirous of emulating the example of the boy Jones'. A writer in the *Irish Independent* claimed that Pike had been lucky, since 'guards are much more numerous than when the boy Jones was such a frequent intruder. He left the mark of his boots on the Sovereign's bed and was behind a sideboard during an audience that Queen Victoria granted to some of her Ministers.'[3]

Queen Mary, who had been in immediate danger of encountering the prowler George Pike back in 1914, had another narrow escape in 1950, when she was living in Marlborough House, situated in Pall Mall, not far from St James's Palace. In July 1950, the burglar Gerard O'Brien decided to break into Marlborough House. Having gained entry through a window, he went into the room of the housekeeper, Mrs Alice Knight, and threatened her with a penknife to make her tell where the valuables were. Although Mrs Knight was sixty-six years old, she was not disposed to surrender without a fight. After she had cried out for help, the elderly assistant housekeeper, Mrs Winifred Ralph, joined the struggle. Since other members of the household, and a policeman on the beat, were also on their way, the burglar had to beat a hasty retreat. Poor Mrs Knight had been stabbed eight times and Mrs Ralph had received a couple of hard knocks in the face. Lord Claud Hamilton, the Comptroller of Queen Mary's household, led a search of the bedrooms and grounds, followed by a large troop of uniformed and plain-clothes police, and reinforced by various royal servants. The police arrested the burglar O'Brien, who was later sentenced to eight years in prison for his cowardly assault on the two old ladies. The eighty-three-year-old Queen Mary had been fast asleep in her bedroom all night.[4]

A *Times* leader writer was most indignant when commenting on these outrages.[5] Clearly, a royal bedroom in the heart of London, patrolled by sentries from the Brigade of Guards and watched over by the police, ought to have been a safe haven for the Queen Dowager. What if this dangerous burglar had gone into Queen Mary's room instead, and threatened her with his lethal penknife? The spectacle of a comptroller directing a search party down into the basement, while the Queen Mother was sleeping upstairs reminded the writer of some remote chapter of history, like the depredations of 'the "boy Jones" who, a fortnight after the birth of Queen Victoria's first baby, declared that he had spent three days in the Palace, hiding under beds and helping himself to soup'.

From the 1920s until the 1950s, there had been a few instances of tramps or lunatics straying into the Buckingham Palace grounds, but they had always been swiftly apprehended. Throughout the 1960s and 1970s, the royals at Buckingham Palace remained unbothered by palace intruders. It would appear as if comparatively little money was spent on security during these years. For each year that went by, the royal guardians became more careless, and their routines increasingly slack. Although Buckingham Palace had a good alarm system, it was not superior to that of any country house owned by a wealthy magnate, and the sheer size of the palace was enough to impede the swiftness of any police response. In 1981, there were three incidents suggesting that the guarding of the palace grounds left much to be desired. In June, three German tourists were discovered camping in the gardens; when challenged by the sentries, they said they were under the impression they were in Hyde Park. In August, a lunatic was discovered hiding in some bushes; when challenged, he said he had been looking for Princess Anne. In December, another lunatic was apprehended inside palace grounds. Still, it would not appear as if these uninvited visits resulted in any improvements to palace security.

Early in the morning of 9 July 1982, all seemed well at Buckingham Palace. When Queen Elizabeth II woke up, she was surprised to see some individual drawing back the curtains. At first, she thought it was a servant and angrily asked 'Who are you?' since she was not supposed to be roused at such an early hour. But then she saw that the man in her room was a wild-looking character, dressed in jeans and a dirty old T-shirt; he was cradling a broken ashtray and dripping blood on the royal bedlinen from a badly lacerated hand. Although it must have been quite an effort, her Majesty managed to keep her calm. She promptly called the palace switchboard, asking them to summon the police. But although the operator did pass the message through to the palace police office, they did not respond.

Sitting down on the royal bed, the palace intruder said that his life had not been pleasant in recent times. His original plan had been to commit suicide in the Queen's bedroom, although he had changed his mind 'since it would not be a very nice thing to do'. Sensing that the intruder was certainly neither a terrorist nor an assassin, but a confused young man, the Queen kept him talking about his family affairs. The intruder found it a remarkable coincidence that they both had four children. When he asked her for a cigarette, the Queen readily acquiesced, seeing an opportunity to get rid of her mysterious visitor. She pressed a button to summon the chambermaid, but nobody came. She then called the palace switchboard, but there was again no response from the police.[6]

Although the palace intruder had made no hostile move whatsoever, the situation must have been fairly desperate. But when the Queen had spent ten minutes with the disturbed, bleeding intruder, a chambermaid suddenly entered the bedroom. On seeing the wild-eyed intruder sitting on the royal bed, she exclaimed the memorable words 'Bloody hell, Ma'am! What is *he* doing here?' in her strong Geordie accent, before running out to alert one of the footmen, who was just returning after having walked the corgis. The confused intruder made no resistance when he was grabbed and pushed into a pantry by this individual. Puffing at the cigarette he had belatedly been given and sipping from a drink fetched for him by another polite footman, he told the royal servants that they should treat him with respect, since he was in fact none other than Herr Robert Hess, son of the notorious Rudolf. The police finally arrived twelve minutes after the Queen's first call and took the palace intruder into custody. When manhandled by the police, the intruder became angry and abusive, telling the constables what he thought of them in no uncertain manner, before being dragged away from the presence of royalty.

When he was taken into custody, the intruder turned out to be unemployed Irish labourer Michael Fagan. This was not the first time he had visited Buckingham Palace; in fact, he was awaiting trial for being apprehended outside the palace a month earlier, grasping half a bottle of cheap white wine that had been sent as a present to Prince Charles by some well-wisher. Fagan had stolen this bottle somewhere in the palace, and had taken some drinks from it to refresh himself, just like the Boy Jones had enjoyed the royal ham and potatoes. There was also the matter of a young housemaid who had seen a 'Peeping Tom' spying on her in her quarters at Buckingham Palace. Had this been Fagan? At the time, the police had established that the young woman had been to a spiritualist séance the same evening, and they suspected she might have been 'seeing things', but forensic experts had found an unidentified set of fingerprints on the window-sill. Fagan freely admitted this previous visit to the palace, adding that it had been great fun to sit on the throne swigging from the Prince's bottle of Johannesburg Riesling.

Just like in the original Boy Jones scandal, the authorities did their best to hush up the Michael Fagan incident. They thought it would be embarrassing for the Queen to read about her nocturnal meeting with Fagan in the newspapers, and there was a general feeling of shame that an intruder could have entered Buckingham Palace with such consummate ease. But some disloyal servant or police constable leaked the story to both the *Sunday Mirror* and the *Daily Express*. The *Mirror* thought the whole thing was a hoax, but the *Express* had some clever journalists investigate the story closely, before splashing this great scoop across its Monday headlines.[7] The astute journalists even noticed that the Fagan episode was in fact 'a remarkable repeat of an incident at Buckingham Palace 142 years ago when a boy burglar was found hiding in Queen Victoria's dressing room, a few feet from where the young Queen was sleeping.'

Now the cat was among the pigeons, to the embarrassment of the royal household, police and government alike. After all, this was the time the Provisional IRA were exploding bombs in London. Had Fagan been a terrorist, he could have killed the Queen with the greatest of ease, before running off to settle the scores with the remainder of the royal family, and blowing up what remained of Buckingham Palace with a powerful bomb. Prime Minister Margaret Thatcher had to make an official apology to the Queen, and Home Secretary William Whitelaw faced angry and ribald questioning in the House of Commons. The politicians took out their anger on the bumbling royal guardians. The first head to fall was that of Commander Michael Trestrail, head of the Royal Protection Squad, after it had been divulged he had a homosexual relationship with a male prostitute. Sergeant Cyril Hunt, a fifty-five-year-old police veteran who had been in charge of the palace police office the night Fagan broke in, was suspended, and two palace police constables were transferred to other duties.[8] It was never explained why the police had been so very tardy in responding to the summons from their Sovereign: had the officer taking the call thought it was a practical joke, or had he been sleeping on duty?

According to a 'fictionalised biography' of the Queen, Her Majesty acted with commendable coolness when facing the palace intruder. She first called the palace telephone operator asking for 'tea' but the operator thought it was a joke and wanted to double-check with one of the royal maids, who did not answer the phone. When calling the second time, the Queen also asked for 'a policeman' but again the dim-witted operator failed to follow his Sovereign's command. He merely phoned the palace police office for some advice, and was told by the duty officer that he would indeed notify someone when more officers came on duty.[9]

The more scholarly biographies of Queen Elizabeth II have had nothing to say about these alleged shenanigans, however. One of them instead mentions that the Queen told her former press secretary 'that she got out of bed, put on a dressing-gown, drew herself up to her full regal height and said "Get out!" but he did not.' According to the same source, she later told a friend that the whingeing Fagan 'just talked the usual sort of bilge that people talk to me on walkabout. I can handle that.' On a harsher note, a royal footman, who had heard the Sovereign deliver a fair dressing-down to the bungling palace policemen after the Fagan incident exclaimed, 'I have never heard the Queen so angry!'[10]

With Fagan behind bars at Brixton Prison, the police tried to reconstruct how he had entered Buckingham Palace. It turned out that the agile intruder had climbed a 14-foot wall topped with spikes and barbed wire, injuring his hand in the process. An off-duty policeman had seen him scale the wall, but when he had alerted the palace police, they were unable to spot the intruder. Fagan walked on to the west side of the palace, where he found an open window and climbed in. This was the room housing King George V's stamp collection, worth more than 5 million pounds, but since Fagan was no stamp fancier and the door to the corridor securely locked, he went back outside through the window. An alarm had been triggered when Fagan entered and exited the Stamp Room, but the policeman on duty thought it was malfunctioning and turned it off both times.

Fagan then walked undetected all the way round the palace. On the east side, he climbed up a drainpipe and entered the unlocked office of Vice Admiral Sir Peter Ashmore, who was responsible for the Queen's security. He then strolled along the corridors for a considerable period of time, admiring the paintings and making excursions into various rooms. In one of them, he picked up a glass ashtray as a souvenir but promptly dropped and broke it, again cutting his hand. He passed a royal housekeeper, who politely said 'Good morning' to the barefooted, scruffy intruder, before entering the Queen's unguarded bedroom.

The normal routine was for an armed police officer to stand guard outside the Queen's bedchamber until 6 a.m., at which time he would be replaced by one of the footmen. But on the morning in question, it would seem that the tired police sergeant had just strolled off, without waiting for the footman, who was busy walking the Queen's corgis. Not unreasonably, these slack routines arose widespread public outrage. How could the palace police just turn off alarms that had been triggered, and why did they not answer the Queen's call for help with some urgency? How many of them had been sleeping on duty that fateful night? And was it really right that the life and safety of the Sovereign should be entrusted to an elderly policeman, who clearly did not take his duties very seriously, and a twenty-two-year-old dog-walking footman?

By the time of the Michael Fagan incident, there was a considerable police presence at Buckingham Palace: a superintendent, an inspector, two sergeants and twenty constables. But according to the assistant editor of the *Police Review*, interviewed by a *Times* journalist, the police duties at the palace were not considered very arduous. Many of the constables were close to retirement age, others ambitious youngsters who took advantage of the slack routine to study for their promotion exams. In the past, their performance had been found wanting on regular occasions. Once, some jolly constables had taken some time off to go paddling in the goldfish ponds. More seriously, a constable supposed to be on duty outside the Queen's bedchamber had been discovered in bed with a maid.[11]

In the meantime, Michael Fagan senior, father of the palace intruder, held court at the Grosvenor public house in Islington.[12] Clutching a pint of lager in one hand and a treble Scotch in the other, this paunchy, jolly-looking old chap announced to the assembled Fleet Street journalists that there was to be an auction for the exclusive rights to his son's amazing story. He titillated them with some spicy stories: for example, Michael had often spoken of his lovely new girlfriend Elizabeth Regina, who was a bit older than he was, but whom he liked to visit as often as he could!

The irrepressible *Sun* newspaper was of course unable to resist the temptation to take the Fagans on board: on 13 July, they could present their grand World Exclusive about the crazy palace intruder who thought the Queen was his girlfriend.[13] According to his father, Michael Fagan had gone into the palace at least twelve times to see his beloved Elizabeth Regina. His first words to her had been 'you are very beautiful and I love you very very much!' They had enjoyed a long conversation, and the amorous Fagan had found her entirely delightful, although he had noticed she had pins in her hair and was not wearing her wig.

On 14 July, Fagan's wife Christine provided another exclusive for *The Sun*. She knew for sure that her estranged ex-junkie husband was deeply in love with Elizabeth Regina and had visited her bedroom several times. Since he spoke about her at length, in the most glowing terms, Christine first thought he wanted to make her jealous, but now it sent shivers down her spine when she realised he was speaking of the Queen herself! She had visited her husband in prison, finding him in good cheer, although he had just been examined by a psychiatrist. Fagan's mother struck a sadder, and much more truthful, note when she added that her son's mental balance had always been very fragile. The previous month, he had stabbed his stepson in the neck with a screwdriver, and just two weeks before, he had tried to slash his own wrists. She presumed that her brave son had been appalled by the lax security around Buckingham Palace and sacrificed himself to make people aware that the Queen was in great danger from lunatics and terrorists.

There were mixed reactions to these tabloid press shenanigans.[14] The British morning papers were derisive, suggesting that the disreputable Fagans had milked the situation for every penny it was worth, with complete disregard for the truth. The American and Canadian newspapers were more gullible and readily regurgitated stories from *The Sun* and *Star*. The Japanese had a particular fascination for the Fagan scandal: the story of the Queen's uninvited guest hit the headlines of the *Asahi* and other leading Japanese newspapers.

With Fagan safely behind bars, Director of Public Prosecutions Sir Thomas Hetherington was considering what charge was to be made against the palace intruder. Just like in the days of the Boy Jones, trespass was still a civil, not a criminal, offence, but it would at least be possible to charge Fagan with the theft of the wine bottle. Importantly, it also turned out that Fagan was already awaiting trial for two other incidents. Firstly, he had stolen a Ford Cortina; secondly, he had stabbed his stepson during a drunken argument. The car owner was willing to press charges, the stepson more reluctant to do so, either from step-filial affection or from fear of further ill-usage when the palace intruder got out of jail.

When Michael Fagan was taken to the Bow Street magistrates' court on 19 July, he seemed in a good mood, like if he enjoyed being the centre of attention.[15] A short, wiry young man with curly hair, he smiled benignly and gave his family a cheerful wave. He was charged with three offences: stealing a bottle of wine during his first visit to Buckingham Palace, stabbing his stepson, and stealing the car. Fagan chuckled to himself when a senior police detective opposed bail, with the motivation that the palace intruder was a very disturbed man, with serious personal problems and suicidal tendencies. Instead, he got angry when his own solicitor, Mr Maurice Nadeem, mentioned the incident with the Queen, shouting that he had already sacked the solicitor several times and that he would rather plead guilty than have her name blackened. When Michael Fagan senior stood up to speak on his son's behalf, Michael junior announced, 'That man is not my father. My father is Rudolf Hess.'

Michael Fagan went on trial at the Old Bailey on 23 September, before the Recorder of London, Judge James Miskin.[16] Mrs Barbara Mills was prosecuting and Mr Richard Slowe defended the palace intruder. Fagan was respectably dressed and did his best to behave accordingly, addressing everybody in court as 'Your Worship', even the ushers. But when the prim-voiced Mrs Mills was addressing the jury at length, the palace intruder tried to annoy her by taking out his dentures and making a loud mewing noise. The Judge glared at him and said, 'If you are going to make that sort of noise, we will continue this case without your presence.'

After re-inserting his 'snappers', Fagan politely replied, 'I promise I will behave, Your Worship. I won't do it again.'

There was more buffoonery when Fagan was called to testify himself. After contemplating what religious persuasion he belonged to, he finally chose 'Atheist' and read out the relevant oath in a sonorous voice, beginning with the instruction at the top 'Please read out your name clearly'. He again freely admitted climbing up the drainpipe, stealing the wine bottle and frightening palace housemaid Sarah Carter. She was the prettiest girl in court, according to a susceptible *Daily Mirror* reporter, and Fagan courteously apologised to her, saying that he was very sorry for giving her such a fright. He was very keen to testify also about his second visit to Buckingham Palace, when he saw the Queen, but this was not allowed. Mr Slowe skilfully described Fagan as a confused individual wanting to have a look at Buckingham Palace, and accidentally 'finding' the wine in a cupboard, and the jury sentenced him 'Not Guilty', since no intention to steal had been proven. Fagan leapt to his feet and gave a 'V' sign to his parents and sisters. But Mrs Mills was not done with him. He sullenly pleaded 'Guilty' to stealing the car and was taken back to Brixton Prison.

There was of course outrage in the press that the palace intruder had been let off so very lightly. When questioned by journalists, Home Secretary William Whitelaw had to admit that the law of trespass was old-fashioned and did nothing to protect the homes of the rich and famous from burglars, lunatics and various other unwanted visitors. When Fagan was back in court on 4 October, the authorities had hoped to persuade his stepson to give evidence against him, but since the lad had gone abroad to escape them, the assault charge fell through when he failed to turn up in court.[17] Still, the authorities were better prepared this time. Two psychiatrists, Dr Edgar Unwin, the medical director of Broadmoor, and Dr George Grant, the medical officer of Brixton jail, testified that Fagan was a very disturbed and unstable man who was a danger to the public in general and the Queen in particular. Thus Fagan was sentenced to be held indefinitely in a top-security mental hospital, for the single offence of stealing a car. Not at all unreasonably, Fagan banged the wall of the dock and shouted, 'The palace is fitting me up!'

A few days later, Fagan was removed to Park Lane mental hospital in Liverpool, where he soon became known as 'King Cuckoo'. There were regular news bulletins about his life behind bars.[18] In October, a brawny young lunatic named Philip Baxter, who had become an inmate after attacking two old men with an axe, decided to pick a fight with Fagan. But the palace intruder had a snooker cue handy and used it to good effect, knocking the would-be axe murderer out cold. Fagan's wife Christine, who seems to have been almost as dotty as her husband, moved in with a nineteen-year-old builder, leaving her brother Kenny to take care of her numerous brood of children. He soon tired of this task and threatened to have the children taken into care. In late December, Michael Fagan senior again appeared in the tabloids, complaining that his son was not allowed to attend Catholic worship. Cardinal Basil Hume promised to make sure this was properly investigated.

In January 1983, Michael Fagan was finally freed from the mental hospital, after he had convinced a tribunal he was fit to be released. When his volatile wife, who had kicked out the younger man she had been living with, took Fagan back, there were emotional scenes when the palace intruder saw his children again.[19] Fagan fancied himself as a singer and joined forces with a punk band called *The Bollock Brothers*. Together with them, he recorded a cover of the Sex Pistols' *God Save the Queen* that was released as a single and is said to have made the charts. Fagan T-shirts were sold in King's Road, Chelsea, and his promoter made plans for him to give concerts in Madrid and the United States, before going to sea just like the Boy Jones, to become the star musical performer on board the liner *Queen Mary* on its forthcoming cruise round the world. But when Fagan made his debut at the Ba t punk club in London, he was booed off the stage. A fearsome-looking punk with pink and blue hair spat at the palace intruder for 'murdering' his favourite anthem. The punk rocker population of London continued to show their disapproval of Fagan's renditions of the Sex Pistols' songs in such a forthright manner that his tour was cut short and the release of a second single with a cover of *Pretty Vacant* put on hold indefinitely.[20] At another punk club, Fagan got drunk and started fighting with three men, headbutting two of them in true punk fashion before punching the third in the face. Unfortunately for him, they turned out to be plain-clothes policemen, and he was put on probation for assault, as well as being forced to attend a psychiatric outpatients clinic.[21]

As the palace intruder was amusing himself in the London punk clubs, the politicians debated whether the law of trespass should be changed. After Home Secretary William Whitelaw had ordered a review of the law of trespass, there was prolonged legal wrangling. A Home Office report suggested that either there should be a complete overturn of the old law, making 'simple trespass' into any person's house a criminal offence, or this protection should only be given to royal residences. Both these solutions were problematic: the first one would make criminals of small boys retrieving footballs from the lawns of neighbours; the second would expose Mrs Thatcher's government to the obvious criticism that it protected the homes of the royals, but neglected those of ordinary people. In the end, Tory peer Lord Onslow introduced his 'Criminal Trespass on Residential Premises Bill', also known as 'Fagan's Law' to the House of Lords. The Fagan incident had shown the law as it stood to be an ass, he pontificated: even the most undesirable form of trespass could be committed with impunity. Since every Englishman's home should be his castle, there was a need to protect all these premises from unwanted intruders, from the royal palaces to the most humble of council homes. But in spite of Lord Onslow's efforts, there was a lack of enthusiasm for his bill. Civil liberties organisations asked about the status of people straying into private property by mistake and questioned how 'intent to trespass' would be defined. And would the police have power to enter people's houses to remove trespassers? In the end, the bill came to an ignominious end in July 1984, and the old law of trespass remained.[22]

In July 1984, Michael Fagan hitch-hiked to Wales to get away from all the pressures of London life. But due to his heavy drinking, the trip was not a success. In a Fishguard café, Fagan became furious when the owner asked him to turn his transistor radio down, expressing himself in strong language and adding some observations about the Welsh national character. When two locals tried to evict him, a scuffle began, in which Fagan soon held the upper hand. A third man, who just happened to be a plain-clothes policeman, tried to intervene, but was greeted with a well-aimed blow in the eye from the palace intruder. Fagan was arrested, convicted of four counts of assault, and jailed for a month.[23]

In October 1984, when Fagan was living with his family in a ramshackle Holloway flat, an insane woman set fire to the flat below. Showing considerable bravery, Fagan led his children to safety before returning to tackle the blaze with blankets and buckets of water. The fire brigade praised his actions, and it was thought he might be awarded a medal.[24] Fagan's next newsworthy exploit came in August 1987, when he was fined £150 for indecent exposure after a woman motorist had seen him running about without trousers on waste land in Chingford, Essex.[25] In February 1992, Fagan gave an interview to a South African newspaper, talking at length about his troubled life.[26] He lived in a squalid North London flat, taking care of his three children after his wife again had left him, this time to join a hippy commune. Just like the Boy Jones, Fagan at length lamented his unwanted notoriety: 'It seems there is nowhere I can go without some joker asking me if I've heard from the Queen!' He graphically described how he had sneaked into the Throne Room, taken off his shoes and socks, and sat on each of the thrones. The Queen had been very calm, he asserted, just pressing the alarm bell and telling him to get out.

When appearing in Radio 4's appositely named 'Famous for Fifteen Minutes' show on 25 March 1993, Fagan reiterated the truthful version that all the Queen had said to him was 'What are you doing here?' and 'Get out!' He had made a record and tried to build a cabaret act around his notoriety, he said, but success had eluded him, and he was now a full-time father and grandfather.[27] But it seems as if Fagan's life gradually went downhill during the 1990s, particularly after he had become a heroin addict. In December 1997, he was jailed for four years for dealing heroin from his squalid Islington flat; when he was sentenced, it was mentioned that he had multiple previous convictions for assault, dishonesty and possession of heroin.[28] In 1999, he proudly posed for a *Daily Mirror* photographer in his tiny prison cell, holding a caricature of the Queen smoking a joint with the text 'Chill out!'[29]

In 2001, Fagan was back in his native town of Derry, Northern Ireland. The local tourist board got wind of this and advertised that visitors to Derry might have the opportunity of meeting the man who had once sat on the Queen's bed, if they were lucky. Fagan is said by the same authority to have become quite popular, never having to pay for a pint again.[30] In early 2006, he was back in Holloway, North London, with a new flat and a new girlfriend. He boasted to a journalist about sitting on the throne swigging from Prince Charles's bottle of South African Riesling, this time adding that the wine had been so very nasty he did not finish it. He had become a firm royalist, he asserted, and hoped the Queen would live to become a hundred years old. He wished to apologise about any fright he might have caused her Majesty, and particularly that he had urinated in the corgis' food bowl just before entering the royal bedroom. It had been a naughty thing to do, he admitted, but the situation had been a desperate one and no other receptacle had been at hand. He had now given up both drink and drugs, he claimed, and the journalist found him both sprightly and amusing.[31] Let us hope that the life of this bizarre reincarnation of the Boy Jones has continued in the same benign manner, and that if he decides to visit Australia, he takes good care not to fall asleep on a bridge after he has had a few too many.

The Michael Fagan incident had the positive effect that royal security was considerably improved. Millions of pounds were spent on reinforcing the garden walls, adding spikes and barbed wire, and installing an up-to-date alarm system. The palace police was reinforced and more officers were on duty during night-time. The corrupt system of regarding duties at Buckingham Palace as some kind of sinecure for elderly constables came to an end: they were replaced by younger, tougher colleagues, who had special training in responding to the intricate alarm system.

In the years to come, the Buckingham Palace security system was tested at regular intervals by various disturbed individuals who thought they had reasons to come and visit the Queen. As a rule, these intruders were swiftly captured by the palace police. One woman thought the Queen was her mother; a young lunatic claimed that there had been a mix-up of babies at the maternity ward and that he was really Prince Andrew; an amorous Irishman had travelled all the way from Dublin after falling in love with a deceitful woman who had told him she was the Queen's niece.

A more serious threat for the royal guardians came in July 1992, when the twenty-one-year-old drifter Darryl Marcus successfully scaled a wall near Constitution Hill, ran across the lawns, and clambered through an open palace window. The half-naked, desperate intruder remained at large for two and a half minutes, before he was caught at gunpoint by armed police just at the door of the Queen's private apartments on the first floor. Although a nasty customer, alleged to have previous convictions for violent crime, Marcus was released without charge and transported back to a homeless shelter in Peterborough. Already being on bail for throwing a brick at a car and assaulting a security guard, he was later convicted and imprisoned for these offences. When interviewed in the newspapers, Marcus said he had entered Buckingham Palace as a protest, although he was not entirely certain about what.[32]

The reason this rebel without a cause had got as far into the palace as he did was that he had scaled the wall and ran across the lawns with great speed. Although the palace police had picked up the alarm straight away, the agile intruder had outrun them. There was to be further embarrassment in July 1993, when a group of female anti-nuclear protesters dashed out of a van, put some aluminium stepladders up against the Buckingham Palace wall, and cut a hole in the fence on top of the wall.[33] All fifteen women made it to the palace lawns, where they chanted slogans and waved banners standing just twenty yards from the royal apartments. They were all arrested and frogmarched into a fleet of police cars. Tory MP Sir Teddy Taylor expressed indignation, claiming that, in 1992, there had been thirty-two attempts to break into the four main royal palaces. He demanded that every palace intruder should receive an automatic jail sentence.[34]

In 2003, *Daily Mirror* journalist Ryan Parry managed to obtain a job as a Buckingham Palace footman using a false reference. He could roam the palace at will, serve food to the Queen and other lofty personages, and take photographs of the Queen's bedroom and the bedroom President Bush was to use on a coming state visit. Although many people were outraged that the Queen had been waited on by a snooping journalist, the *Mirror* got a great scoop. The newspaper could rightly claim that Parry had exposed glaring faults in the vetting of royal employees. For example, a simple Internet search would have revealed that Parry, who was using his own name, was quite a well-known Fleet Street journalist.

Prime Minister Tony Blair's New Labour government showed more resoluteness in dealing with these shortcomings than his rival Margaret Thatcher had done twenty years earlier. Firstly, security was upgraded and the archaic routines for checking the references of applicants for jobs within the royal household revised. Secondly, influential judge Dame Elizabeth Butler-Sloss was appointed to chair a commission to improve security for the royal family, senior politicians and various other magnates considered to deserve special protection.

The members of the Royal Security Commission received a hurry-up when, in September 2004, two protesters advocating the rights of divorced fathers decided to make a stunt at Buckingham Palace. Dressed up as Batman and Robin, they climbed a high fence and ran swiftly across the grounds. Although his trusty sidekick was arrested by armed police, the Caped Crusader made it all the way to the palace, where he climbed the balcony and hung up a large banner saying 'Super Dads of Fathers 4 Justice'. The policemen tried their best to persuade this ludicrous figure to climb down from the ledge he was perched on, but Batman stayed there unmolested for five hours; he waved merrily to the onlookers when he was finally taken on board a large crane that the police had purposely set up to capture him.[35] This pathetic sight was the last straw for the authorities. As usual, Batman could not be charged with any offence; as usual, the newspapers were outraged. But not long after the palace intruder had driven his Batmobile out of court, the Royal Security Commission was ready to change the ancient law of trespass to prevent further outrages of this kind.

The Serious and Organised Crime Police Act of 2005 makes it a criminal offence to enter certain royal palaces, government buildings, nuclear sites and military bases. When a burglar was arrested in the back offices of No. 10 Downing Street in June 2007, it was thought he would have the honour of becoming the first person to be prosecuted under this new law, but embarrassingly, it turned out that someone had forgotten to put up the requisite warning signs and the burglar escaped prison as a result.[36]

11

What Was Wrong With the Boy Jones?

Unlike Oxford I dreamt not of shot at our Queen,
Within ear-shot content, so I could not be seen;
And I'faith the taste's good, though Paul Pryism's shabby,
To see her Majesty's self and her infantine babby!

From *The Era* of 28 March 1841

Before addressing the question what was wrong with the Boy Jones, there are a few other mysteries to be pondered. Firstly, what can be ascertained about how many times he entered Buckingham Palace? We know that he was apprehended in the act three times. He had also admitted another brief intrusion, just prior to his second visit; that time, he had calmly left after perceiving that many people were about. There are many circumstances suggesting that these four visits were not the only ones, however. We know that already in December 1838 he navigated the palace with the greatest of ease. How could he have known the layout of the palace so well if he had never been there before? Now, Buckingham Palace was (and is) a vast and labyrinthine structure, without any helpful signs pointing out the Queen's private apartments, the Throne Room, the kitchen and other interesting sites to visit for the enterprising palace intruder. Yet both in 1838 and in 1840, the Boy made his way to the Queen's private apartments without much difficulty; nor did he fail to visit the Throne Room, or to retrieve victuals from the kitchen. We may only speculate, but perhaps the Boy's claim to have spent around twelve months in the palace referred to his first paying Her Majesty a visit twelve months before he was captured in December 1838? His behaviour in 1840, after he had lost his job, must also be viewed with the greatest suspicion: when he absented himself from his family, was this not to sneak into Buckingham Palace, spend a few days in there spying on the Queen, and then make his way out again without being detected? The conclusion can only be that, from 1838 until 1841, the Boy Jones probably entered Buckingham Palace many times; during three of these visits, he was discovered, but in other instances he escaped scot-free.

The second mystery is by what means the Boy Jones got into Buckingham Palace. Here, we are on somewhat firmer ground, since from his own admission, he twice entered the palace through an unshuttered lower-ground-floor window in December 1840. Lord Duncannon's investigation clearly showed that, for once, the Boy was telling the truth: there were telltale signs that he had broken through an unsecured window, and then entered the servants' quarters through an unlocked door. The laxity of Buckingham Palace security was such that nothing would have prevented him for making use of this winning formula again, and again, and again.

There are some rival theories as to how the Boy got into the palace. Firstly, some people at the time suggested that he came in through the chimney. But although the Boy had the habit of making some of his outings to Buckingham Palace in December, there is no evidence he chose the same perilous mode of entry as that attributed to Father Christmas. During daytime, it would not be possible to climb up the palace roof to get to the chimneys without being detected; during night-time, such a climb would have been near-suicidal, considering the slippery roof and tall chimneys. There is no reason to doubt the expert chimney sweep who declared it impossible to get into the palace through any of the chimneys, since they had been purposely constructed to make this impossible. Even the story that the Boy might have been hiding in the chimneys during the daytime is hard to believe, due to the obvious risk of him being suffocated or even roasted alive.

Another contemporary theory was that the Boy had an accomplice inside the Palace. According to *The Times*, many people, among them the Boy's father, were of the opinion that one of the royal scullery-boys let the Boy Jones in through the palace kitchen entrance in Pimlico.[1] This hypothesis was based on the extremely slender evidence that, when arrested in March 1841, the Boy was eating a large helping of cold meat and potatoes, which he must have procured in the kitchen. This, the ill-informed journalist confidently states, 'would have been impossible for him to have done if he had scaled the wall, as is supposed, on Constitution-hill'. But this journalist ignores that the Boy had previously, in December 1840, entered the palace through scaling the wall and getting in through a lower-ground-floor window, and later made his way to the kitchen to get some victuals. He also ignores that, when captured in March 1841, the Boy's shoes were quite wet and muddy, something that is consistent with him scaling the wall and sneaking through the garden, rather than being let in through the kitchen entrance. And would such a loner as the Boy Jones really trust one of the scullery-boys to help him, and what motive would such an accomplice have to aid and abet the palace intruder? The conclusion must be that there is no evidence whatsoever that the Boy Jones entered Buckingham Palace by any other route than through one or other of the unsecured lower ground floor windows.

A third curious question is what Queen Victoria herself thought of the Boy Jones. As we know from her journal, she originally considered him a half-witted chimney sweep who had 'only come to see the Queen', but she admits she would have been very frightened if she had come face to face with him. There are two other records of the Queen's reaction to the Boy Jones, both taking place many years later. In 1865, the Queen returned to Coburg for Prince Albert's birthday. Later, at a dinner in January 1867, 'the Queen referred to the old days at Buckingham Palace & the boy Jones whose feats from her account would not be needful to obtain access at Coburg where a petitioner from the street knocked at her dressing room door ...'.[2]

When Sir Henry Ponsonby, Queen Victoria's private secretary, was having dinner at Balmoral in November 1873, he sat next to the Queen. After Lady Erroll had told a story about a robber found concealed in a house, Sir Henry asked the Queen about the Boy Jones: 'She said she never saw him. She was recovering from the birth of the Pss Royal and he seems to have hid himself in the room in which she sat in the day time – but he was caught when she was not there. She thinks he was a petty pilferer but had no preconcerted ideas of robbery and got in more for the fun of the thing than anything else.'[3]

Several authors have made more or less well-informed deductions what was wrong with the Boy Jones. In his brief account of the palace intruder, published in 1948, crime writer Horace Wyndham thought him 'altogether, an odd youth. Nowadays, if he appeared in court, he would stand a chance of being sent to Vienna for psycho-analysis.' The first historian to make a serious effort to find out more about the Boy Jones was Mr John Woodiwiss. But although his 1950 book was entitled *Mad or Bad?*, Woodiwiss abstained from making any diagnostic prediction regarding the Boy's sanity. The psychiatrist Dr Hubert Norman, who contributed a long preface to this book, was much more confident, stating that the Boy was an individual 'of a psychopathic type', suffering from 'an obsessional condition (neurosis).' Just as some people had a fixation with leading with the right foot when crossing the street, Norman claimed, the Boy Jones could not control his urge to enter Buckingham Palace. In 1967, the coroner and medico-legal expert Gavin Thurston wrote a short article on the Boy Jones, in which he concluded that, although the Boy was of a 'peculiar and curious nature', there was no evidence he was actually insane. In contrast, octogenarian solicitor Leonard le Marchant Minty, writing in 1985, considered the Boy little better than a halfwit.[4]

When contemplating these wildly divergent opinions, the first step has to be to assess whether Minty was right. Was the Boy Jones an imbecile? No, certainly not! I think the reader of this book would agree. He could read and write, and he had a voracious appetite for even the most unpromising reading material, like old newspapers and scrap paper. The journalists who attended the examinations at Bow Street in 1838 thought the Boy quite clever and

quick-witted. His employer Mr Griffiths testified in court that the Boy was
certainly 'very clever' but of a haughty and indolent disposition; when he
made an effort, he could be a good and reliable worker. As we recall, Serjeant
Adams himself spoke of the Boy's 'superior talents' that could elevate him
to a much higher position in life if properly applied. The *Weekly Chronicle*
journalist described him as very inquisitive, always thirsting for information.
Even Inspector Evans, albeit a dubious source, 'spoke in high terms of the
boy's intelligence and good conduct'.[5] As we know, the Boy Jones was clever
enough to learn the layout of Buckingham Palace like the back of his hand
and to outwit the palace guardians repeatedly. No halfwit could have shown
the enterprise and cunning needed for the Boy's depredations at the palace,
and the conclusion must be that he was at least of normal intelligence.

A more promising suggestion is that the Boy might have suffered from
schizophrenia. His own father, his employer Mr Griffiths, and many of the
journalists that interviewed him during the days of his fame, all found him
very odd. His idea that the building of cardboard houses would help him to
become an architect is bizarre, his reluctance to take up the generous offer
to go on stage inexplicable. Why was it so important to him that all objects
on the tea tray should be in perfect order and that his shoes should always
be well polished, while at the same time he neglected his personal hygiene
to such a degree that he became positively repulsive even by Victorian
standards? What was he writing, when he sat before the fire poring over
his sheets of scrap paper, changing and correcting the text again and again:
love letters to the Queen, chapters in his forthcoming book on Buckingham
Palace, or just nonsense? Nobody will ever know, since this extraordinary
Boy always ended his hour-long writing sessions with throwing everything
he had written into the fire, without allowing any person to see it. Like the
majority of schizophrenics, the Boy Jones was a loner; he had no friends, no
confidant even among his own siblings. A gloomy, solitary figure, brooding
and secretive, there is no evidence he showed any particular respect or
affection even for his long-suffering parents. Both 'Paul Pry' and the *Weekly
Chronicle* journalist thought him extremely odd in his behaviour and
mannerisms; in particular, they were amazed how cold and ungrateful the
Boy was to old Henry Jones. The aforementioned officer of the *Warspite*
called the Boy a strange-looking fellow, who appeared half asleep and
seldom spoke to any one.

But to qualify as a schizophrenic according to modern psychiatry, the
individual has to suffer from some kind of delusions and/or hallucinosis.
There is no evidence that the Boy Jones ever suffered false beliefs or
hallucinations; he did not 'hear voices in his head', had normal speech, and
did not suffer from catatonia. His father and most of the journalists who
met him considered him fully sane, although profoundly odd in his intellect
and manners. The naval authorities shared the opinion that he was sane and

fully fit to serve as a seaman. Importantly, the two experienced doctors who examined the Boy in December 1840 did not declare him insane, although they must have been under considerable pressure from the government to do so. Had they given way to this pressure, the Boy Jones would have been put into Bedlam for a very considerable period of time. By comparison, the unfortunate Edward Oxford, who ill-advisedly had used the insanity defence, was locked up in 1840 and not released from Broadmoor until 1868.

There is a condition known as a schizoid personality, where the individual is strikingly withdrawn and solitary, emotionally cold, and lacking interest in social relationships.[6] Its prevalence is less than 1 per cent of the general population. These individuals do not fulfil the criteria for schizophrenia, do not have delusions or hallucinosis, and may well have a normal intelligence. Many of them have odd ideas and compulsions, are proud and reserved, and appear to be indolent, absent-minded and engrossed in fantasy. As we remember, the Boy Jones had a thorough aversion to menial work. Mr Griffiths said he was of a 'proud and ambitions turn of mind, never thinking anything good enough'. Henry Jones told the *Weekly Chronicle* journalist that Edward often said that his father's humble abode was not good enough for him. Although it is of course adventurous to attach a psychiatric diagnosis to an individual who has been dead for more than 100 years, and whose character is preserved only in the words of others, this description fits the gloomy, solitary Boy Jones quite well.

Individuals with a schizoid personality disorder may have secret voyeuristic interests, or even develop erotomania, also known as de Clérambault's syndrome.[7] The shy, introverted patient, who is often an unattractive loner, develops a fixation on some person of the opposite sex, often someone of a much higher position in society. The patient develops a delusion that this stranger returns his feelings and begins pestering him or her with unwanted letters and presents, or becomes a stalker, following the loved one from a distance, or even breaking into his or her house.

A contemporary of the Boy Jones, the French psychiatrist Jean-Etienne Esquirol, described the curious case of an unattached thirty-six-year-old man of melancholy disposition and unprepossessing appearance, who fell desperately in love with a beautiful actress. He tried to communicate with her, approached her repeatedly, and loitered outside the theatre and outside her house. Although she made it clear she wanted nothing to do with him, and although her husband once beat him up badly enough to put him in hospital, he continued to stalk her. When the forthright Esquirol asked him how he could possibly believe she had any interest in such an ugly, penniless nobody as himself, the deluded Frenchman replied, 'All that is true, but love does not reason, and I have seen enough to leave me in no doubt that I am loved.'[8]

In 1920, psychiatrist Gaetan de Clérambault, after whom the syndrome has been named, described another case of erotomania.[9] A paranoid, lonely, fifty-three-year-old French milliner developed the fixed idea that King George V was in love with her and that his secret emissaries were watching her. All London knew of their affair and wanted it to succeed, she believed. She spent large sums of money to travel to England, where she prowled around the royal palaces, although the corpulent, middle-aged Frenchwoman was incapable of repeating the heroics of the Boy Jones to meet her beloved King in the flesh.

Stalking is a serious problem in present-day society.[10] Every literate American knows what a stalker is, although the concept is a modern one. In the 1970s and early 1980s, there was concern about the relentless pestering of women by former partners. This referred to, at the time, as 'female harassment', 'obsessive following' and 'psychological rape'. No person mentioned the word 'stalking' and in spite of the best efforts of the women's movement, there was no change in either legislation or police attitude toward these offenders.

But in the mid-1980s, there was intense media interest in what seemed like a totally different phenomenon, namely the pursuit of celebrities by obsessive fans. The murder of actress Rebecca Schaeffer by demented fan Robert Bardo showed that these individuals could be deadly. Some clever journalist coined the term 'star stalking', which was an instant success. Not just celebrities but ordinary people as well became seriously worried about being pursued by some crazy person who was capable of murder and rape. The 1987 blockbuster film *Fatal Attraction* added fuel to these worries: the worst nightmare of many Americans was to be followed and monitored by some potentially violent, deranged person. The very word 'stalking', with its sinister promise of pursuit and imminent violence, caught people's imagination. American domestic violence campaigners expanded the term to cover not only celebrities, but also ordinary women being pursued and harassed by violent ex-partners. Since there was widespread public outrage, the same legislators who had not bothered much about 'female harassment' swiftly introduced anti-stalking laws in all US states. Europe and Australia were to follow.

In the 1990s, many psychiatrists and social scientists took an interest in this epidemic of stalking that seemed to sweep the globe. This led to the medicalisation of stalking: a realisation that the stalkers were not just plain evil, but often themselves quite unhappy, disturbed individuals. There were praiseworthy efforts to classify the stalkers, in an attempt to learn more about what kept their abnormal behaviour going. A large group of stalkers were pursuing a former partner who had rejected them; others were paranoid individuals who had developed a grudge against some person who had annoyed them, starting a vendetta that sometimes went on for years; some were people (often men) who simply were socially incompetent and who could not fathom that the women they desired wanted nothing of their attentions. A smaller group consisted of dangerous predatory stalkers, who were often paedophiles or perverts of other descriptions. They chose their victim and stalked him or her to plan the perfect assault or kidnapping. Another large group of stalkers consists of intimacy seekers, who develop an obsession with some person, and a desire to get to know him or her better.[11] Some of them chose humble victims: the secretary falls for her office manager, the repressed spinster working for the local charity becomes obsessed with the vicar, and the unemployed young loner becomes infatuated with his social worker. Other intimacy seekers have higher ambitions in life: they become celebrity stalkers, sometimes choosing their victims from among the highest in the land. There is a strong association between this group of stalkers and the patients with erotomania discussed in the previous section; the cases described by Esquirol and de Clérambault would today both be classified as intimacy-seeking stalkers; the Frenchwoman who was obsessed with King George V would also be considered as a celebrity stalker.

There are several modern cases of patients with erotomania stalking celebrities.[11] Some of them are intimacy seekers who stop at nothing to get close to their idols. Twenty-one-year-old Athena Ronaldo had developed an obsession with Hollywood actor Brad Pitt. Although her letters to him had not been answered, she decided to break into his mansion to try to meet him face to face. Doing a 'Boy Jones' to perfection, this agile young woman scaled the high wall and climbed in through an open window. She had a meal of Brad Pitt's gourmet food, wore his clothes and slept in his bedroom, remaining in the residence for ten hours before a housekeeper discovered her and called the police. In court, she seemed a benign character, showing remorse for her foolish actions. As a result, she was not harshly dealt with: a restraining order, three years of psychological counselling, and a few weeks community service in a graffiti-removal scheme. These measures seem to have had the desired effect, and Pitt was free from his stalker.

Margaret Mary Ray was a more determined stalker. In the late 1980s, she became obsessed with talk-show host David Letterman. She claimed he was her husband and the father of their child, once stole his Porsche, and seven times broke into his Connecticut home. Diagnosed as suffering from schizophrenia, she was finally sentenced to ten months in prison for harassing Letterman. This period of incarceration seems to have ended her obsession with Letterman, to the talk-show host's relief, but this sinister woman transferred her affections to retired astronaut Story Musgrave and pursued him relentlessly for several years, finally ending up behind bars for a second time. After being released in 1998, she committed suicide.

President Bill Clinton had his own celebrity stalker, known as 'Jane Doe'. She sent him letters, flowers and presents, and visited various presidential sites. Although receiving no encouragement from the President, she decided to take things further. She legitimately gained access to several presidential fundraisers and more than once shook Clinton's hand. After she had breached the secure perimeter surrounding the presidential limousine, holding a mobile phone, she was committed to a hospital.[12]

Not all celebrity stalkers are as relatively benign as these three, however. It happens, more often in males than in females, that the deluded stalker gets the idea that his ideal woman may not be as pure and chaste as he presumed, or that she is having an 'affair' with someone else.[13] This can turn him resentful and paranoid, sometimes with fatal results. In 1986, demented stalker Robert Bardo shot and killed actress Rebecca Schaeffer, since he had become disillusioned after seeing a movie portraying her in bed with another actor. In 1995, Robert Dewey Hoskins, who had been stalking pop diva Madonna for months, broke into her garden and tried to overpower a security guard. He was himself shot by the guard and later sentenced to ten years in prison. John Hinckley Jr., who had been stalking actress Jodie Foster, tried to gain her affection by shooting and nearly killing President Ronald Reagan in 1981. Hinckley still remains in a secure psychiatric unit.

There are several obvious similarities between these cases of intimacy-seeking, erotomanic stalkers and the Boy Jones. But there are also differences. Firstly, the Boy seems to have been obsessed both by the glories of Buckingham Palace in general and by the Queen herself in particular. Although he sneaked into her private apartments at least twice, once stole her underwear, and another time spied on her from underneath a sofa in her dressing room, there is no evidence he tried to follow her around, or to break into Windsor Castle as well. Secondly, although stalking behaviour has been observed in adolescents, it is usually on a local or domestic level.[14] The bespectacled 'nerd' might fall in love with the school beauty and follow her around, and the 'plain Jane' might do the same to the captain of the football team. Although it is common that teenagers admire celebrities like actors and sports stars, they tend to do so from a distance. There are very few, if any, examples of young teenagers becoming celebrity stalkers and breaking into their houses. The medico-legal and psychiatric literature is unable to come up with anything even resembling a fourteen-year-old Boy stalking a nineteen-year-old Queen. The conclusion thus must be that in spite of the advances in criminology and psychiatry, the Boy Jones remains unique and unclassifiable.

Although stalking is regarded by most as a modern problem, the annals of stalking-like behaviour stretch far back into time.[15] Authorities on stalking have highlighted Dante Alighieri's obsession with Beatrice and Petrarch's infatuation and idealised love for Laura. This may be fanciful, since we do not know to what degree the lovesick Italian poets actually persecuted their ideal women. The Danish philosopher Søren Kierkegaard, whose behaviour was sometimes more than a little odd, wrote a quaint collection entitled *Enten-Eller* (*Either/Or*), part of which was *Forførerens Dagbog* (*The*

Seducer's Diary). In this weird story, the narrator systematically spies on, pursues and manipulates a young woman. He gathers information about her and engineers 'accidental' meetings in public places. *The Seducer's Diary* is likely to be partly autobiographical and based on Kierkegaard's obsessive love for Regine Olsen, to whom he was engaged for a while. In the 1840s, when Kierkegaard published his book, *The Seducer's Diary* was seen as an amusing and picaresque tale, but modern commentators have made a more sinister interpretation of its main theme.

Another early literary treatment of stalking-like behaviour comes from an unexpected source: Louisa May Alcott. In her Gothic novel *A Long Fatal Love Chase*, written in 1866 but not published until 1995, the heroine Rosamond marries the sinister Philip Tempest.[16] It does not take long for her to realise that he is a cruel scoundrel and a bigamist at that. She escapes to Paris, but the demented Tempest pursues her. Rosamond assumes various disguises: a Parisian seamstress, a governess in Germany, and even a nun in a convent, but each time Tempest pops up when least expected, ruining her prospects. He keeps stalking her for two years, telling her he enjoys the sport. Rosamond falls hopelessly in love with a Roman Catholic priest, who tries to help her to escape back to England, but Tempest is hot on their heels. Hoping to murder the priest, he rams what he perceives to be his boat, but it turns out that he has killed Rosamond by mistake. Grasping her lifeless body, he stabs himself, exclaiming, 'Mine first – mine last – mine forever!'

Stalking-like behaviour was not encountered in literature alone. In 1704, the physician Dr Lane was pursuing Miss Dennis, a wealthy heiress. She did not care for him, and her mother forbade him to contact her, but the determined doctor kept entering their house, trying to seek out Miss Dennis. Mother and daughter fled to London, but the doctor followed them. He beat up a man who was escorting them, and later thrashed their solicitor with a cane. Dr Lane was charged with assault, but since he was a wealthy and respectable physician, the violent doctor escaped with providing £400 as a security for keeping the peace and, in particular, not contacting Miss Dennis for a year and a day. Nothing can be deduced about the success, or lack of it, of this measure.

A most audacious and persistent stalker, and a contemporary of the Boy Jones, was the Irish barrister Richard Dunn. In 1838, when staying at Harrogate, he met the twenty-four-year-old Miss Angela Burdett-Coutts. The year before, she had inherited her grandfather's fortune of nearly £2 million, making her the wealthiest woman in England. Although Richard Dunn was a middle-aged man, he fell violently in love with her, and believed his feelings were reciprocated. This was far from being true, however, since the prim young lady found him both forward and uncouth. After he had written her some very indecent letters, her father called in the police and Dunn was imprisoned in York Castle.

In December 1838, Angela Burdett-Coutts was back in London, and so was Richard Dunn. He knocked at the door of her father, Sir Francis Burdett, and demanded to see her. This not being granted, he took lodgings at the Gloucester coffee house in Berkeley-street, selecting a room that had a good view of Miss Angela's bedroom window. Not content with just spying on her, he several times approached her carriage. As *The Morning Chronicle* expressed it, 'where Miss Coutts walked, Mr Dunn walked behind her, and when she rode, he attended on horseback'. Having some private means, Dunn could afford to be a full-time stalker, and since he daily became more forward and impertinent, Angela Burdett-Coutts feared for her life. Her father again called in the police, who posted a constable by the Burdett front door and warned Dunn about his foolish conduct. But since the stalker did not relent, he was arrested on Christmas Eve and brought before the Bow Street magistrates.[17]

Dunn was most indignant, objecting that there must be a conspiracy against him. He was ordered to find sureties of £500 to keep the peace, and to stay away from Angela Burdett-Coutts for a year. But complaining vociferously, Dunn grabbed a poker and began waving it around in a dangerous manner. The constables overpowered him and he was imprisoned in Tothill-fields Prison. In the newspapers, there were references to Mr Dunn's 'many amusing freaks' and the whole thing was seen as a joke; there does not appear to have been much sympathy for Angela Burdett-Coutts, who had been so relentlessly stalked. In Tothill-fields, Dunn bragged that he was not through with the wealthy heiress, and that he would marry her one day. It is not known whether another prisoner, a short and dirty boy, whistled nonchalantly when he heard the Irishman's braggadocio, before exclaiming, 'Pooh! That's nothing! Now hear who *I* have set my sights on ...'

When emerging from Tothill-fields in early 1839, Richard was not Dunn with Angela Burdett-Coutts, not by any means. Despairing of getting rid of 'Miss Coutts's Suitor', as the newspapers called him, by legal means, Sir Francis Burdett tried illegal ones. After Dunn had followed them to Reigate, Sir Francis hired four ruffians to give him a merciless beating. But still the stalker did not give up. In June 1840, he was pursuing Angela Burdett-Coutts and her friend Miss Meredith along Hanover-terrace, near Regent's Park. Seeing that the two ladies were quite frightened, homeowner Mr Alexander interceded, letting them into his house and refusing to admit the persistent Dunn. The police were called, Dunn arrested, and later sentenced to provide £200 in securities for keeping the peace.[18] But in spite of the inability of the legal system to do something about an offender of this kind, wheels were in motion to put an end to his career. Sir Francis Burdett was determined to get rid of his daughter's stalker, and in 1841, he was imprisoned in Newgate for perjury, trespass and failure to pay his bail.

Due to the Burdett family's influence, Richard Dunn was kept in Newgate until August 1846. But he emerged from prison as determined as ever. He had developed the idea that Angela Burdett-Coutts had promised him her hand in marriage, and £100,000 as well. She had made the promise in writing, but unfortunately he had lost the original letter.[19] She had also sent him the following indecent poem, he alleged:

Send to Coutts your bill –
There's lots in the till –
I'll give the clerk orders to do it,
Then get your discharge,
Your dear body enlarge,
And in Stratton-street let me view it.

And, by the bye, love,
My affection to prove,
For your long cruel incarceration,
Fill a good round sum in
(As I've plenty of tin),
To make you a fair compensation.

But Angela Burdett-Coutts was not amused by the stalker's re-emergence, and he was again prosecuted for perjury, ending up in Newgate for another eighteen months. In August 1853, he was in the Insolvent Debtor's Court. Although he read some more poems, which he called 'Sparks from Miss Angela's heart', he was sentenced to ten months in jail. With much feeling, Dunn screamed that he wanted to die, and that he hoped that his gravestone should have the inscription 'Murdered by Miss Angela Burdett-Coutts'.[20]

In 1856, this demented stalker was still active, however, although the subject for his perverted affection had changed: Dunn was now obsessed with the twenty-three-year-old Princess Mary of Cambridge. Perhaps he thought Angela Burdett-Coutts, who was now forty-two years of age, had become too old for him, or perhaps he wanted to emulate his former prison mate, the Boy Jones, and go after royalty. Dunn sent the princess a number of impertinent letters, and went to St James's Palace to speak to one of her maids. The princess informed the court authorities about these weird letters, and they called in the police. Dunn was promptly arrested and brought before Bow Street magistrates.

When questioned, Dunn said that the princess had once given him 'an unmistakable look of recognition' when she had passed him in an open carriage. Although he was pursued by the daughter of a marquis, who desperately wanted his hand in marriage, and although his Bury-street landlady was continually pestered by the servants of ladies of distinction enquiring about him, he instantly knew that the young princess was the girl for him. Even Queen Victoria herself fancied him, he asserted, but although the palace door had been thrown open to him, he purposely avoided going that way.

Richard Dunn knew that his feelings for Princess Mary were fully reciprocated, since he had seen two young women in Bond-street, and he was instantly convinced they had been sent by the princess to look out for him. When he had visited St James's Palace, he had been sure that the princess was waiting for him upstairs, and that she would have come down to join him, had she not been prevented by the servants!

After this insane outburst, some of Dunn's indecent letters to Princess Mary were read aloud in court. Two experienced doctors, who had examined Dunn while in custody, both declared that he was of an unsound mind and labouring under certain delusions. The verdict was that he was not a person of sound mind and that he should be placed under restraint in an asylum.[21] Nothing is known about his eventual fate.

In 1883, unemployed solicitor Edward Rowdon became infatuated with the young heiress Violet Lane-Fox. Although both Miss Lane-Fox and her mother Lady Conyers made it clear that she wanted nothing to do with Rowdon, who was nearly twice her age, he relentlessly followed her around. He found out which parties they were going to, and obtained an invitation himself to be able to pester them. Lady Conyers took her daughter to Europe to escape the bugbear Rowdon, but he followed them there, behaving as obnoxiously as ever. Once, he threw himself down in front of Lady Conyers, to demand her daughter's hand in marriage. Since he kept tracking them from town to town in Germany and Switzerland, they had to return to London.

In vain, various male relations of Lady Conyers tried to bribe, threaten or reason with Rowdon. But in the end, the stalker was unwise enough to write a letter to Miss Lane-Fox, threatening to shoot her unless she agreed to meet him in private. This gave Lady Conyers the opportunity to prosecute him. The 'Extraordinary Charge of Annoying Ladies' arose a good deal of newspaper ridicule; should Miss Lane-Fox not in fact be flattered to have such a persistent admirer? The court took a sterner and less flippant view of things, however, and in September 1885, Rowdon was sentenced to six months in prison.

Emerging from jail as determined as ever, Edward Rowdon started following Miss Lane-Fox around just like before. When he optimistically inserted an advertisement in the *Morning Post*, announcing his impending marriage to Miss Lane-Fox, Lady Conyers and her solicitors struck again: in June 1886, the stalker was prosecuted for criminal libel, and sentenced to eighteen months in prison. The judge called him an unmanly scoundrel and was sorry he could not add hard labour to the sentence. Still, this harsh sentence seems to have had the desired effect, since nothing was heard about Rowdon annoying Lady Conyers or Miss Lane-Fox again.

In 1890, the aspiring young actress Louisa Pounds began studying at Gunn's Metropolitan School of Shorthand. One of the other students, unemployed clerk Alexander Edwin Sharpe, was very much taken with her good looks. He had been in the habit of pestering a certain Miss Collins, but now he transferred his attentions to Louisa Pounds. He followed her around, tried to get alone with her, and made her some very impertinent suggestions. After Miss Pounds and Miss Collins had complained to the headmaster, the bugbear Sharpe was dismissed from the school.

The sinister-looking Sharpe kept following Louisa Pounds about, however, and wrote her some very disagreeable letters. In one of these, he actually threatened to shoot her. When Miss Pounds and her friend Mr Gunn came to challenge the demented Sharpe, he pulled out a large revolver and screamed, 'I will either blow out your brains, or my own!' Being seriously frightened of what her sinister 'admirer' might be capable of, Louisa Pounds went to the police, and in November 1890, Sharpe was charged with threatening to shoot her. His barrister did not deny that Sharpe had threatened to murder Miss Pounds, but he pointed out that his client had always been very foolish and eccentric, and that his respectable family were much ashamed of him. Sharpe's brother promised to take him to Australia, where he would no longer be able to annoy Louisa Pounds. The judge sentenced him to a year in prison, however.

But in the tradition of the determined stalkers described earlier in this chapter, Sharpe did not give up. Emerging from prison as mean-spirited as ever, he was very much dismayed to see that his victim's career had blossomed: under the stage name Louie Pounds, she was now a celebrated actress at the Prince of Wales' Theatre. In March and April 1892, she several times saw Sharpe's ugly face grinning at her from the theatre audience and received some very impertinent and threatening letters from him. After he had threatened to disfigure her using vitriol, Sharpe was again taken to court; this time, his family's suggestion that he should be given a one-way ticket to Brazil was acted upon, and Louie Pounds was free from her stalker. She went on to become quite a famous actress, active until the 1930s and living to be nearly a hundred years old. It is not known whether Sharpe found any nice Brazilian ladies to stalk after being 'transported' to South America.[22]

A striking American example of a violent celebrity stalker concerns ace baseball player Eddie Waitkus. He had distinguished himself as a soldier in the Second World War, before becoming a famous baseball professional. His biggest fan was young Chicago clerk Ruth Ann Steinhagen, who went to all his matches and collected hundreds of newspaper clippings and photographs of him. Her parents were more than a little worried about her infatuation with Eddie, particularly since she sometimes said the best thing was for her to shoot first Eddie and then herself, since she loved him so very much. They paid for her to see two psychiatrists, but neither was able to do anything for her. Ruth Ann Steinhagen objected to Eddie playing for Philadelphia after being sold by the Chicago Cubs, since she could now only see him play when the Cubs played the Phillies at home. Before one of these matches, in June 1949, she downed a couple of whiskies, before sending Eddie a message that she wanted to see him in her hotel room. When he appeared, she shot him in the chest with a small-calibre rifle. She was certified insane and incarcerated in an asylum. Miraculously, Eddie's life was saved, and he went back to playing baseball, but he became a changed character, worried and morose, seeing trigger-happy, demented fans everywhere.[23]

The cases of Dr Lane, the Boy Jones, Richard Dunn and the other two Victorian stalkers discussed above clearly demonstrate that stalking definitely is not a modern phenomenon, rather a new categorisation of a form of aberrant human behaviour that has been around for centuries. There are clear parallels between the Boy Jones, the Frenchwoman (described by de Clérambault) who was in love with George V, and that other palace intruder, Michael Fagan. The demented Richard Dunn, who stalked Angela Burdett-Coutts for fifteen years before turning his attentions to Princess Mary of Cambridge, was a nineteenth-century kindred spirit to the sinister Margaret Mary Ray, who stalked David Letterman and the astronaut Story Musgrove.

The laws of these times were wholly incapable of dealing with a stalker: the violent and unbalanced Dr Lane seems to have escaped scot-free back in 1704. Since the Boy Jones's trespass into Buckingham Palace was not a criminal offence, illegal methods had to be resorted to in order to get rid of him and remove the threat to the young Queen. Initially, Richard Dunn also escaped prison, and the newspapers considered his ceaseless persecution of Angela Burdett-Coutts as harmless pranks, but the wealth of Coutts's bank seems to have played a not unimportant role in his eventual downfall. In the end, when he transferred his perverted courtship to Princess Mary, his fate was sealed, and it seems as if he ended his days in an asylum.

12

What Was Wrong With Lord Melbourne & the Government?

If I was his father, I'd break all his bones
Or send him to sea, like that *other* Boy Jones!

J. R. Planché, *The Golden Fleece* (1845) [a tirade against Cupid]

The rulers of many European countries found ways of getting rid of unwanted subjects without being hampered by legal concerns. If the Boy Jones had sneaked into Queen Marie Antoinette's bedroom, or if he had been found spying on Napoleon and his Empress underneath a sofa, a *lettre de cachet* would have had him imprisoned without charge or trial, perhaps later to end up as a galley slave. Had the Boy intruded on the Tsarina of Russia, he might have received a one-way ticket to the dreaded Siberian prison colonies, or 'disappeared' forever into some hidden dungeon.

But in contrast to the resources possessed by these continental autocrats, whatever ambitions the kings and queens of England may have had to imprison their subjects without trial have been severely impeded by the tradition of *habeas corpus*. This cornerstone of democracy, beginning with the Latin words *habeas corpus* (you may have the body) protected the individual against arbitrary detention by the state and gave any person detained the right to appear before a court of law for the legality of the imprisonment to be determined. The original writ of *habeas corpus* predated the Magna Carta; the law was formally passed by Parliament as the Habeas Corpus Act of 1689.

The Habeas Corpus Act has been suspended only under the most extreme circumstances of war or civil unrest.[1] It was set aside by William Pitt to arrest various revolutionaries after France had declared war on Britain in 1793. During the Great War, the Defence of the Realm Act of 1914 enabled the authorities to detain without trial people of German descent and also Irish nationals suspected of involvement in the Easter Uprising. In 1939, Defence Regulation 18B again made it possible to round up aliens and suspected saboteurs. In May 1940, when the Germans were at the English

Channel, and when the example of Quisling had been set, Regulation 18B was hurriedly amended to enable the government also to intern known Nazi or Fascist sympathisers without trial. Soon after, Sir Oswald Mosley and the most fanatical of his Blackshirts were rounded up and jailed, along with a motley crew of German nationals, collaborators and suspected traitors. In 1971, the British Government introduced the internment without trial of hundreds of republican suspects in an attempt to defeat the IRA. Since this scheme was far from a success and actually recruited further support for the Irish nationalists, it was abandoned four years later. Finally, in our own times, the terrorist outrages committed by Muslim fanatics have prompted the Prevention of Terrorism Act of 2005, giving the government the right to detain foreigners suspected of terrorism without charge or trial for a certain period of time.

It would seem well-nigh insane to compare, even for a moment, a young pauper boy with a mania for entering the Queen's palace, without being armed or having any violent intent, with sinister German saboteurs, blackshirted Fascists, gun-toting IRA men and demented Muslim terrorists. But as we know, the scheme to get rid of the Boy Jones also set aside the Habeas Corpus Act. In addition, the Boy was actually kidnapped by government agents during peacetime and sent on board a merchant ship against his will. Then he was kidnapped for a second time, this time to be shanghaied on board a man-of-war. He served as a sailor against his will for more than five and a half years, thus being unlawfully detained for longer than any alien saboteur, Blackshirt or terrorist.

So why was Lord Melbourne's government so very frightened of the Boy Jones? As we know, his first palace intrusion back in 1838 had been treated more or less like a joke. But since then, there had been two sinister developments. Firstly, the radical Chartist movement had gained momentum, culminating in the Newport riots of 1839. The Chartists demanded wholesale parliamentary reform and abolishment of the Poor Law. They freely criticised the Queen, since they were disappointed that living conditions for the poor had not improved since her accession, and some of them were republicans. Secondly, the Edward Oxford assassination attempt made the Queen and government aware that there were deranged and desperate people out there who had the intent to harm her. Just like Oxford, the Boy Jones was young, impoverished and very odd. He also had the uncanny ability to enter Buckingham Palace at will and to find his way to the Queen's private apartments. Since the law was an ass and simple trespass into a royal palace not a criminal offence, the Boy could come and go as he wanted, as long as it could not be proven that he had any intent to steal.

For each of the Boy Jones's intrusions into Buckingham Palace, the pressure on Lord Melbourne's government grew. Attempts to persuade the Boy to become a seaman or to emigrate failed, and when he emerged from jail in June 1841, a plan had been hatched to have him abducted by illegal means. This plan had certainly been approved by Lord Melbourne and Lord Normanby, and quite possibly by Queen Victoria herself. Whoever conceived this plan seems to have thought that there were two good ways of making a person disappear without going to the extremes of murdering or secretly imprisoning them. Either the Boy could be sent to the colonies, preferably Australia or New Zealand, or he could be shanghaied on board ship as a sailor. The *Diamond* emigrant ship seemed to offer both these possibilities, but the resolute opposition from the irascible Captain Taylor ruined this plan. Instead, the Boy was shanghaied on board a merchantman, but only to return to London half a year later. Since the threat to the Queen was still present, another, better plan was concocted, quite possibly with the involvement of the Captain of the *Warspite*, Lord John Hay. In times of war, until the defeat of Napoleon, it had been perfectly legal to kidnap mariners, or even landsmen, to force them to serve as sailors in the Royal Navy.[2] Why not bring back impressment, just for one day, and just for this meddlesome palace intruder? As we have seen, this second plan had the desired effect. Although the Boy Jones made at least two attempts to escape, he had to serve as a sailor in the Royal Navy from early 1842 until early 1848. There is good evidence that he was never allowed on shore unguarded and that the utmost care was taken to keep him in the Mediterranean region, far from London and Buckingham Palace.

As we have seen, there was some contemporary opposition to the cruel and illegal methods used to dispose of the Boy Jones. At first, the Tory papers had blamed Lord Melbourne's government for allowing the Boy to enter Buckingham Palace, and they urged that the palace intruder ought to be flogged and transported. They made a *volte-face* after the Boy Jones had been disposed of, however: since they realised there might be some public sympathy for the poor Boy who had been so shamefully treated, they used him as a tool to attack the Whigs. Was it really right that a publican and a police inspector should be allowed to abduct a young boy and shanghai him on board ship? But although this newspaper assault must have annoyed Lord Melbourne and his government at the time, it was of short duration and did the Boy Jones little good. The Tory newspapers lost interest after the change in government in late 1841, and only a few liberal-minded enthusiasts, like Charles Dickens, questioned the legality of kidnapping the Boy and packing him off to sea. There is some evidence there was sympathy for the Boy Jones among the poor people of London, but nobody listened to them.

It is hard, however, not to have some sympathy for Lord Melbourne's government, since he and Lord Normanby were really in an impossible position. The Boy Jones was odd and unpredictable, he could enter Buckingham Palace at will, and there was no legal way of getting rid of him. Nobody knew what was going on in the Boy's twisted mind. What if he had decided to kill his faithless Queen after her marriage, or to shoot his 'rival' Prince Albert? If the Boy Jones had turned into a royal assassin, like the equally odd Edward Oxford, the newspapers would have blamed the government for not getting rid of him, although he had thrice signalled his intent to do mischief. Lord Melbourne and Lord Normanby would have been the most hated men in the country for failing to protect the young Queen, and it is very likely the entire government would have had to resign.

To have been clandestinely kidnapped and spirited away without charge, in breach of the Habeas Corpus Act, and to be the last person impressed as a Royal Navy sailor in recorded history are not the Boy Jones's only claims to fame in legal history. As we know, he was twice tried by the Privy Council, like if he had been some rebel earl in the time of Queen Elizabeth I. The reason for this archaic machinery to be utilised to try a young pauper boy was almost certainly the fear of what lewd and scandalous revelations (true or false) the Boy might make of his observations inside the Queen's private apartments. To prevent these matters becoming public, a secret court had to be used. This controversial move from Lord Melbourne's government was widely criticised by the Tory newspapers at the time. Amazingly, it has never since been repeated: the Boy Jones remains the last person tried *in camera* by the Privy Council on a charge clearly within the jurisdiction of a magistrate.[3]

After her accession to the throne, there was immense public curiosity about Queen Victoria, and all aspects of her life at Buckingham Palace. The books and pamphlets about her exaggerated her personal attractions: not only was she good and noble, but also superlatively beautiful. The early portraits and prints of her also showed her as a beauty. As a result, many young men fell in love with her. Some threw letters into her carriage, a few tried to visit her; the most persistent admirer was the Boy Jones, who persecuted her for at least three and a half years.

The Boy Jones was a character that appealed to the Victorians: a pauper with a dream, a waif in wonderland. He comes across as a weird, asexual Peter Pan, whose fantastic adventures are seen, fleetingly, through the eyes of others. His life certainly had its ups and downs. From the chandeliers and marble halls of Buckingham Palace to the stinking cells and grinding treadmill of Tothill-fields; then back to the palace, back to prison, shanghaied to sea, and then back to London again, only to be kidnapped a second time.

When was the spirit of the Boy Jones broken? When did he realise there was no light at the end of the tunnel? When did the proud Boy Jones, who had dreamt of improving his lot in life, anointed himself with the bear's grease of royalty, and twice sat on the throne, become the feeble, impotent Man Jones: a drunken nobody just like the father he had once so despised? His life after leaving the navy does not appear to have been a particularly pleasant one, but a steady decline into crime and alcoholism. He seems to have remained faithful to his beloved Queen; at least, no contemporary source mentions any interest in the opposite sex at any stage of his later career. His dismal experiences as an unsuccessful burglar demonstrate little of the audacity and determination shown by the young Boy Jones, and it seems as if his main pleasure in life came from drinking to excess.

It cannot have helped that the Boy Jones carried his unwanted notoriety with him, like an albatross tied around his neck, for the remainder of his life. When he had been in London, he could not go outdoors without being mobbed by a crowd of guttersnipes who called out, 'There goes the boy who heard the Princess cry!' On board the *Warspite*, everybody knew who he was, and it made his life miserable to be the butt of every facetious joke. In Fremantle, his attempt to hide behind an alias soon fell through: the other convicts and townspeople all knew about the Boy Jones who sold hot pies, and he was notorious once more. When he was Town Crier of Perth, the children teased him beyond endurance with their incessant impertinence. Even in Bairnsdale, during the final years of his life, his drinking companions knew his true identity. He would die alone underneath a bridge.

The tale of the Boy Jones is a story of extremes: the high and low, rich and destitute. If the Boy had really met the Queen face to face, what would have happened? Would he have spoken about his cardboard houses and his dreams of becoming an architect, asked for some quotations for his forthcoming book about life at Buckingham Palace, or just gazed at his sovereign like a lovestruck mooncalf? And would the Queen have met his gaze, horrified, like if he had been an escaped warthog from Wombwell's menagerie?

Notes

PREFACE

1. Notable biographers of Queen Victoria who have mentioned the Boy Jones include L. Strachey, *The Illustrated Queen Victoria* (London, 1987), 94; D. Creston, *The Youthful Queen Victoria* (London, 1952), 301-2; E. Longford, *Victoria R.I.* (London, 1987), 154-5; and S. Weintraub, *Victoria* (London, 1987), 151-2, 333.

2. The error of two different Boys (Cotton and Jones) appears to have originated in C. Woodham-Smith, *Queen Victoria* (London, 1972), Vol. 1, 217-8, and is further elaborated by P. Wright, *The Strange History of Buckingham Palace* (Stroud, 1999), 167-8, and S. Weintraub, *Albert* (London, 1998), 114-5; the latter book adds the further invention that the Boy was declared insane.

3. There were nineteenth-century accounts of the Boy Jones in *All the Year Round* 34 [1884], 234-7 (reprinted in *Littell's Living Age* 5s, 47 [1884], 443-6), *Newcastle Weekly Chronicle*, 16 August 1884 7c, and *Lloyd's Weekly London Newspaper*, 27 November 1892 9e. There have also been a number of brief modern accounts of the Boy Jones, the best of which are by J. Ashton, *Gossip in the First Decade of Victoria's Reign* (London, 1903), 70-6, 148-57, H. Wyndham, *This Was the News* (London, 1948), 9-12, J. Woodiwiss, *Mad or Bad?* (London, 1950), 108-27, G. Thurston (*Contemporary Review* 210 [1967], 250-7), L. le Marchant Minty (*Medico-Legal Journal* 54 [1985], 29-39), S. Poole, *The Politics of Regicide in England* (Manchester, 2000), 202-4, and M. Diamond, *Victorian Sensation* (London, 2004), 13-15.

4. 'Paul Pry', *Royal Secrets, or a Pry in the Palace* (London, 1841), 4.

1 THE SWEEP IN THE PALACE

1. On the capture of the palace intruder, see *The Times* 15 December 6f and 17 December 7e; also *Police Recorder* 16 December 1838 4a. Bear's grease was, at the time, wrongly presumed to stimulate hair growth on balding pates.

2. On the media image of the young Queen Victoria, see the articles by J. Plunkett (*Critical Survey* 13 [2001], 7-20, and *Media History* 9 [2003], 3-18); also his book *Queen Victoria, First Media Monarch* (Oxford, 2003), 133-9.

3. C. Hindley, *The Life and Times of James Catnach* (London, 1878), 304.

4. *Spectator*, 28 June 1838, 600.

5. M. House and G. Storey, *The Letters of Charles Dickens* (Oxford, 1969), Vol. 2, 23.

6. National Archives, MEPO 2/44.

7. On Lynden and Tucker, see also Poole, *Politics of Regicide*, 177-83, and *London Dispatch*, 4 February 1838.

8. On Captain Goode, see *The Times*, 6 November 3a, 7 November 3f, 13 November 5c and 24 November 1837 2d, and *Illustrated Police News*, 24 February 1883.

9. *Bristol Mercury*, 18 November 1837; National Archives MEPO 2/44.

10. *Ipswich Journal*, 14 July 1838; *London Dispatch*, 9 September 1838; National Archives MEPO 2/44.

11. Woodham-Smith, *Queen Victoria*, Vol. 1, 261-3; E. Healy, *The Queen's House* (London,

1997), 145-51; C. Hibbert, *Queen Victoria: A Personal History* (London, 2000), 137-41.

12. On the various examinations of Edward Jones, see *The Observer*, 17 December 1838 3d; *The Times*, 19 December 5b, 20 December 7b and 22 December 1838 5a; also the *Operative*, *The Era* and *Police Recorder* of 23 December 1838. The early quotations are all from the *Observer* article.

13. On these police deliberations, see *The Observer*, 17 December 1838 3d.

14. *The Era*, 23 December 1838, 148.

15. *Operative*, 23 December 1838, 127.

16. The 1841 census tells us that the forty-five-year-old William James, landlord of the Bell, was living at the premises with his wife Sarah and fifteen-year-old twins Joshua and Jane. He had crammed fifty-one people into the various buildings in Bell-yard, one of them being the sixty-year-old Henry Jones, born in Clahouse, Herefordshire, and his wife Mary, born in Liverpool, Jamaica. There is no reason to presume that this Westminster slum lord had fewer tenants back in 1838.

17. *The Times*, 28 December 1838 7e.

18. The trial of Edward Jones was most fully reported in *The Times*, 29 December 7c, and *John Bull*, 30 December 1838; also in *The Morning Chronicle* of 29 December, and *The Era* and *Examiner*, 30 December 1838.

19. *John Bull* and *Examiner*, 30 December 1838.

20. *Figaro in London*, 24 December 1838, 130.

21. *Satirist*, 23 December 1838, 405.

22. *Satirist*, 30 December 1838, 416.

23. *Newcastle Courant*, 4 January 1839, 4.

2 THE BOY JONES STRIKES AGAIN

1. *Examiner*, 28 March 1841. It was later doubted whether it really was Fenimore Cooper who had offered the Boy Jones to emigrate or another American with the same name.

2. Poole, *Politics of Regicide*, 181-3.

3. M. House and G. Storey, *The Letters of Charles Dickens* (Oxford, 1969), Vol. 2, 17; Hindley, *Life and Times of James Catnach*, 327.

4. Longford, *Victoria R.I.*, 149-65.

5. On the Edward Oxford affair, see Woodiwiss, *Mad or Bad?*, 128-40, and Poole, *Politics of Regicide*, 183-94; also the articles by R. Moran (*International Journal of Law and Psychiatry* 9 [1986], 171-90), F. B. Smith (*Victorian Studies* 30 [1987], 459-70) and F. R. Freeman (*Journal of Legal Medicine* 22 [2001], 349-73).

6. Longford, *Victoria R.I.*, 155, 286. Kinnaird was a drunken fellow who was later several times demoted within the servant hierarchy, before dying of delirium tremens in 1860.

7. From Queen Victoria's journal in the Royal Archives (RA VIC/QVJ/1840: 3 December), quoted by the permission of Her Majesty Queen Elizabeth II.

8. These matters have been discussed by L. le Marchant Minty (*Medico-Legal Journal* 54 [1985], 29-39).

9. *The Times*, 4 December 5c; *The Morning Chronicle*, 4 December; *Satirist*, 13 December 1840.

10. *The Times*, 4 December 5c and 5 December 4f, *The Morning Chronicle*, 4 and 5 December, and *The Era*, 6 December 1840.

11. Much of this information is contained in a letter from Viscount Duncannon to Lord Melbourne, reporting the results of the examination of the Boy Jones, kept in the Royal Archives (RA MP/3/94), quoted by the permission of Her Majesty Queen Elizabeth II.

12. *The Times*, 5 December 1840 4f; *The Morning Chronicle*, 4 December 1840.

13. *The Times*, 7 December 1840 5a.

14. Hindley, *Life and Times of James Catnach*, 329-30.

15. *Satirist*, 13 December 1840, 390, 394. The word 'darbies' is an old-fashioned term for handcuffs or fetters. A useful overview of the early Victorian satirical newspapers is given by D. J. Gray in *The Victorian Periodical Press* (eds J. Shattock and M. Wolff) (Leicester, 1982), 314-48.

3 RETURN OF IN-I-GO JONES

1. *The Times*, 17 March 1841 6e.
2. *The Morning Chronicle*, 17 March 1841.
3. 'From a correspondent' in *The Times*, 17 March 1841 6e.
4. *The Morning Chronicle*, 17 March 1841.
5. *The Times*, 17 March 1841 6e; *Examiner*, 21 March 1841, 188; *The Era*, 21 March 1841.
6. *John Bull*, 20 March 1841.
7. *John Bull*, 27 March 1841.
8. *Hampshire Telegraph*, 29 March 1841.
9. *Satirist*, 21 and 28 March 1841.
10. *Age*, 11 July 1841, 222.
11. *Weekly Chronicle*, 21 March 1841, 5.
12. Here, Henry Jones was probably bending the truth a little, since the 1838 sources implicitly state that Edward was fired by Mr Griffiths and thrown out by his father, who afterwards regretted his rash action and worried that his son had drowned himself.
13. Reproduced by Woodiwiss, *Mad or Bad?*, 117-9.

4 THE BOY JONES FINDS HIMSELF FAMOUS

1. Hindley, *Life and Times of James Catnach*, 329-30.
2. H. Mayhew, *London Labour and the London Poor* (London, 1851), Vol. 1, 223.
3. M. House and G. Storey, *The Letters of Charles Dickens* (Oxford, 1969), Vol. 2, 246, 265. Later, there was a short article on the Boy Jones in Dickens's old journal *All the Year Round* 34 [1884], 234-37, but this provides nothing new or interesting.
4. C. Dickens, *Miscellaneous Papers*; *Household Words* 15 [1857], 577.
5. *Thomas Raikes's Journal* (London, 1857), Vol. 4, 136.
6. See C. Jerrold, *The Early Court of Queen Victoria* (New York, 1912), Vol. 1, 362. *The Times* of 5 April 1841 6e provides a third version: when asked his name at Tothill-fields, the Boy himself had answered 'with some propriety and much drollery, "In-I-go Jones, Sir"'.
7. *The Era*, 28 May 1841.
8. *Jackson's Oxford Journal*, 25 May 1841.
9. Jarndyce Booksellers, catalogue 69, 2006. Jumbled together with some other radical pamphlets, *Peep in the Palace* by 'E. Jones' is No. 869. This collection, valued at £750, remained unsold when I was kindly allowed to read the Boy Jones pamphlet in late 2008.
10. 'Paul Pry', *Royal Secrets, or A Pry in the Palace* (London, 1841).

5 THE MYSTERIOUS DISAPPEARANCE OF THE BOY JONES

1. *The Times*, 7 July 1841 5f.
2. 'Paul Pry', *Royal Secrets*, 10.
3. *The Times*, 7 July 1841 5f.
4. *The Times*, 11 August 1841 5f.
5. *The Era*, 15 August 1841.
6. E. G. Clancy, *The Overflow of Clancy* (Lane Cove NSW, 1979).
7. *Port Philip Patriot*, 11 November, 29 November and 3 December 1841.
8. His discreditable involvement in the disposal of the Boy Jones does not appear to have done any harm to the career of James Christopher Evans, junior. He was later promoted to superintendent and retired in 1869 after thirty-six years of service in the Thames Police, according to the *Pall Mall Gazette*, 20 November 1869.
9. *The Times*, 11 August 1841 5f.
10. *Examiner*, 24 July 1841, 467.
11. *John Bull*, 17 July 1841, 343, and 14 August 1841, 396.
12. From an unknown newspaper, reproduced by Woodiwiss, *Mad or Bad?*, 120-1.
13. *The Times*, 14 December 1841 5d.

6 SHANGHAIED AGAIN!

1. *The Times*, 14 December 1841 5d.
2. *Examiner*, 18 December 1841; *The Era*, 26 December 1841, 3.

3. *The Times*, 14 December 1841 5d.

4. *Age*, 19 December 1841, 403.

5. *Satirist*, 19 December 1841, 407.

6. *The Times*, 9 February 1842 7a.

7. *The Times* 9 February 1842 7a; *The Era*, 13 February 1842, 3. It is interesting that G. Thurston (*Contemporary Review* 210 [1967], 250-7) claims to have discovered 'A note by the Admiral Superintendent of Portsmouth' that 'records that Edward Jones was to be sent to *Warspite* with a caution that he did not escape' but he unfortunately fails to give details of its whereabouts.

8. *The Times*, 9 February 1842 7a.

9. *Satirist*, 20 February 1842, 62.

10. National Archives ADM 38/8228 and 38/9313.

11. *The Times*, 20 October 1842 5c.

12. *Examiner*, 22 October 1842, 675.

13. *Satirist*, 30 October 1842, 347.

14. *John Bull*, 22 October 1842, 511 and 29 October 1842, 524.

7 BRITAIN'S GALLEY SLAVE

1. *The Times*, 9 July 1844 6g.

2. *Examiner*, 13 July 1844, 434; *Lloyd's Weekly London Newspaper*, 14 July 1844, 9; *Satirist*, 14 July 1844.

3. *The Times*, 9 December 1844 5c.

4. *John Bull*, 18 January 1845, 46.

5. *New Satirist*, 21 November 1841; *Penny Satirist* 29 October 1842, 7 and 28 October 1843, 3 March and 18 May 1844.

6. *Punch*, 6 June 1844, 241, 20 July 1844, 355, and 27 July 1844, 54.

7. National Archives ADM 38/9313.

8. *The Times*, 4 May 1846 5b.

9. National Archives ADM 38/8358.

10. National Archives HO 30/22/5F, ff 58-60.

11. Quoted in *Mariner's Mirror* 26 [1940], 226.

12. *Preston Guardian*, 25 August 1847.

13. *Satirist*, 5 September 1847, 19.

14. *Liverpool Mercury*, 31 August 1847.

15. National Archives ADM 38/8228; *Caledonian Mercury*, 27 January 1848.

16. *Satirist*, 6 February 1848.

17. *Daily News*, 16 October 1848.

18. *The Times*, 20 September 1849 7a; Old Bailey Proceedings online, trial of John Frost.

19. *Lloyd's Weekly London Newspaper*, 30 September 1849; *Satirist*, 6 October 1848.

8 WHAT HAPPENED TO THE BOY JONES?

1. Microfilmed transportation records at the National Archives, Kew.

2. Convict database at www.fremantleprison.com.au.

3. *Derby Mercury*, 2 November 1864.

4. Captain E. F. Du Cane in *Bentley's Miscellany* 51 [1862], 513-27. According to the Oxford DNB, Du Cane served in Western Australia from 1852 until 1856, and at no other time, thus providing valuable support that 'John Frost' was really Edward Jones. He later became Major-General Sir Edmund Du Cane, a celebrated prison reformer.

5. *Plymouth and Devonport Journal*, 26 June 1856 8c; *Plymouth Mail*, 2 July 1856 7c.

6. *The Times*, 8 July 1856 10f.

7. *Punch*, 26 July 1856, 39.

8. According to the 1851 census, Henry Jones was still alive, as were his wife Mary, the daughters Elizabeth and Julia, and ten-year-old James. Rather understandably, he was no longer the tenant of Mr James, but lived in Aford Street, Westminster. In 1861, the eighty-year-old Henry Jones could be found at 106 York Street, with fifty-six-year-old wife Mary and the two daughters still in residence. He is not mentioned in the 1871 census.

9. On Mary's dealings with the law, see *Lloyd's Weekly Newspaper*, 7 October 1849, and

Daily News, 9 June 1854. In 1861, she was married to a man named Robert Thompson, and their two-year-old daughter Harriet was living with the old Joneses.

10. *Trewman's Exeter Flying Post*, 30 September 1868.

11. *Derby Mercury*, 8 November 1871.

12. G. Greenwood, *Queen Victoria, Her Girlhood and Womanhood* (London, 1883), 100-3.

13. Sir H. Lucy, *The Diary of a Journalist* (London 1920), Vol. 1, 160. Lucy does not specify in which magazine he had originally published his appeal, but the article was reproduced in the New Zealand newspaper *Mataura Ensign*, 26 May 1900.

14. *The Age* (Melbourne), 17 June 2002.

15. *Bairnsdale Advertiser*, 28 December 1893; inquest details and death certificate received from Mr John Rigg, East Gippsland Historical Society.

16. *London Journal*, 13 October 1866, 240.

17. Reproduced in the *New York Evening Telegraph*, 10 March 1897. For a similar, equally confused theory, see *Daily Mirror*, 9 February 1905, 10.

18. *The New York Times*, 20 March 1910.

19. According to the Broadmoor records in the Berkshire Record Office, Reading.

9 THE BOY JONES IN LITERATURE & DRAMA

1. On Reynolds and *The Mysteries of London*, see the articles by R. C. Maxwell Jr (*Nineteenth-Century Fiction* 32 [1977], 188-213), E. B. Rosenman (*Victorian Studies* 40 [1996], 31-9), M. Diamond (*Dickensian* 98 [2002], 127-38), and J. Plunkett in A. Maunders and G. Moore (eds), *Victorian Crime, Madness and Sensation* (Aldershot, 2004), 15-30.

2. Hindley, *Life and Times of James Catnach*, 329-30.

3. P. Beale (ed.), *A Dictionary of Slang and Unconventional English*, 8th Ed. (London, 1991), 127; J. Green, *Cassell's Dictionary of Slang*, 2nd Ed. (London, 2005), 172

4. Anon., *Fraser's Magazine for Town and Country* 52 [1855], 155. The Latin quotation is adapted from Virgil's Georgics: 'Who has not written about Hylas?'

5. *Dublin University Magazine* 19 [1842], 118-9.

6. *North British Review* 9 [1848], 192.

7. *New Sporting Magazine* 9 [1845], 355, and May 1848, 347.

8. *Journal of the Society of Arts* 2 [1853], 343.

9. *Bentley's Miscellany* 24 [1848], 35.

10. *Fraser's Magazine for Town and Country* 67 [1863], 480.

11. Sala's articles were in *Belgravia* 9 [1872], 203, and *Household Words* 14 [1856], 469-73.

12. Published in *Fortnightly Review* 109 [1921], 882.

13. According to Australian newspaper *The Argus*, 21 August 1920, 8.

14. *The New York Times*, 2 April 1898.

15. *The Speaker*, 6 December 1890, 630.

16. P. Gordon, *The Boy Jones* (New York, 1942).

17. T. Bonnet, *The Mudlark* (New York, 1949). There is a good Wikipedia entry about the Mudlark film.

18. The reason Sky Gilbert called the Boy Edwin rather than Edward was probably that some contemporary newspapers got his name wrong from time to time. From census and Admiralty records, it is clear his name was really Edward Jones.

19. See the *Toronto Star* and the *Globe and Mail*, 11 February 2002, and *Xtra Magazine*, 21 February 2002. Gilbert answered his critics in the *Canadian Theatre Review*, Issue 117, Winter 2004.

10 UNINVITED VISITORS TO ROYALTY

1. Longford, *Victoria R.I.*; Healey, *Queen's House*, 142-153.

2. *Daily Mirror*, 8 June 1914, 3, and 9 June 1914, 3; *The New York Times*, 16 June 1914.

3. B. Graeme, *Story of Buckingham Palace* (London, 1928), 270-271; *Irish Independent*, 9 June 1914.

4. *The Times*, 26 June 1950 2c and 14 July 1950 3d; *Daily Mirror*, 14 July 1950 5.

5. *The Times*, 26 June 1950 5c.

6. The story of Michael Fagan's intrusion is told in the *Daily Express*, 12 July, 1-3, 6-7; *Daily Mirror*, 13 July, 2-3, and 14 July, 1, 14-15; *The Times*, 13 July, 16, and *Newsweek*,

26 July 1983, 38-39.

7. The inside story is told by journalist Norman Luck in *Mail on Sunday*, 19 March 2000.

8. *Daily Mirror*, 16 July, 1, and 20 July 1982, 1-3.

9. N. Davies, *Queen Elizabeth II* (New York, 1994), 307-16.

10. B. Pimlott, *The Queen* (London, 2001), 491, and M. Kiggell & D. Blakeway, *The Queen's Story* (London, 2003), 231-2.

11. *The Times*, 13 July 1982 1b.

12. *Daily Mirror*, 13 July 1982, 3. Old Fagan was a much shrewder operator than the timid Henry Jones, and a 'character' in his own right, having once received a Royal Humane Society certificate for rescuing three children from a fire; later he successfully donated a kidney to his brother in a pioneering operation.

13. *The Sun*, 13 July, 1-3, 6-7; 14 July 1982, 1, 5.

14. *Manchester Guardian Weekly*, 18 July; *The Guardian*, 9 July; *Toronto Globe and Mail*, 16 July; *The New York Times*, 18 July 1982.

15. *Daily Mirror*, 20 July 1982, 2-3.

16. *Daily Mirror*, 24 September, 1-3; *Washington Post*, 25 September 1982.

17. *Daily Mirror*, 5 October 1982, 1.

18. *Daily Mirror*, 11 October, 5; 20 October 1982, 5.

19. *Daily Mirror*, 20 January, 1; 21 January 1983, 7.

20. *Daily Mirror*, 4 June 1983, 7; website www.discogs.com for Fagan's discography. He cannot have been entirely devoid of musical talent, since he provided vocals for three songs in all on the Bollock Brothers' 1983 album *Never Mind the Bollocks* and also featured on one of their live performance bootlegs.

21. *Daily Mirror*, 4 June 1983, 7.

22. *Daily Mirror*, 2 February 1983, 2; *The Times*, 24 March 4e, 2 December 1983 2c. See also the article by P. Vincent-Jones in *Journal of Law and Society* 13 [1983], 343-70.

23. *Daily Mirror*, 14 August 1984, 13.

24. *Daily Mirror*, 17 October 1984, 15.

25. *The Daily Telegraph*, 4 August; *Daily Mirror*, 11 November 1987 22.

26. *Sunday Mail* (SA), 9 February 1992.

27. *Daily Mail*, 30 March 1993; *Glasgow Herald*, 26 March 1993.

28. *Daily Mirror*, 20 December 1997, 19.

29. *Daily Mirror*, 2 December 1999.

30. *Irish News*, 3 October 2001.

31. *Sunday Star*, 16 April 2006.

32. On the Marcus incident, see *Evening Standard*, 17 July; *Daily Mail*, 18 July; *Daily Mirror*, 17 July 1992, 1, and 18 July 1992, 2-3.

33. *Daily Mirror*, 7 July 1993, 2-3.

34. *Evening Standard*, 29 July 1993.

35. Batman was on the first pages of *The Guardian*, *Daily Mirror* and *Daily Express* of 14 September 2004.

36. *Daily Express*, 10 June 2007, 37; *The Daily Telegraph*, 28 March 2008.

11 WHAT WAS WRONG WITH THE BOY JONES?

1. *The Times*, 26 March 1841 4f.

2. N. E. Johnson (ed.), *The Diary of Gathorne Hardy, later Lord Cranbrook, 1866-1892, Political selections* (Oxford, 1981), 28.

3. Letter from Sir Henry Ponsonby to his wife in RA VIV/ADDA36/694, quoted by permission of Her Majesty Queen Elizabeth II. Although he helped himself to some palace memorabilia on his first (?) visit in 1838, the Boy Jones showed no 'pilfering' tendencies during his later visits.

4. These references are from Wyndham, *This Was the News*, 12; Woodiwiss, *Mad or Bad?*, 18; G. Thurston (*Contemporary Review* 210 [1967], 250-7); L. le Marchant Minty (*Medico-Legal Journal* 54 [1985], 29-39). Although Dr Hubert Norman was a well-known psychiatrist in his day, he must have been very old in 1950, and his grasp of the intricacies of the Boy Jones case leaves much to be desired.

5. These references are from *The Era*, 23 December 1838, 148; *The Times*, 20 December 7b; *Weekly Chronicle*, 21 March 1841, 5; *The Times*, 14 December 1841 5d.

6. On schizoid personality disorder, see the articles by S. Akhtar (*American Journal of Psychotherapy* 41 [1987], 499-518) and M. H. Stone (*British Journal of Psychiatry* 162 [1993], 299-313).

7. On erotomania, see the articles by P. Ellis and G. Mellsop (*British Journal of Psychiatry* 146 [1985], 90-5, S. F. Signer (*Journal of Psychiatry and Neuroscience* 16 [1991], 81-90), R. Lloyd-Goldstein in *The Psychology of Stalking: Clinical and Forensic Perspectives* (New York, 1998), 193-212, N. Kennedy *et al.* (*Comprehensive Psychiatry* 43 [2002], 1-6), and G. E. Berrios and N. Kennedy (*History of Psychiatry* 13 [2002], 381-400).

8. Quoted by P. E. Mullen *et al.*, *Stalkers and their Victims* (Cambridge, 2000), 131-2.

9. Quoted by S. F. Signer (*Journal of Psychiatry and Neuroscience* 16 [1991], 81-90).

10. On stalking in general, see Mullen *et al.*, *Stalkers and their Victims*, and D. A. Pinals (ed.), *Stalking* (Oxford, 2007).

11. On the stalking of celebrities, see the articles by R. T. M. Phillips (*Journal of the American Academy of Psychiatry and the Law* 34 [2006], 154-64) and in *Stalking* (ed. D. A. Pinals) (Oxford, 2007), 227-50, G. D. Clancy (*Journal of the American Academy of Psychiatry and the Law* 36 [2008], 68-73) and D. V. James *et al.* (*Journal of the American Academy of Psychiatry and the Law* 36 [2008], 59-67).

12. On these three cases, see the articles by R. T. M. Phillips (*Journal of the American Academy of Psychiatry and the Law* 34 [2006], 154-64) and in *Stalking* (ed. D. A. Pinals) (Oxford, 2007), 227-50; also Mullen *et al.*, *Stalkers and their Victims*, and *The New York Times*, 22 November 1998.

13. Mullen *et al.*, *Stalkers and their Victims*; R. T. M. Phillips in *Stalking* (ed. D. A. Pinals) (Oxford, 2007), 227-50.

14. On juvenile aspects of stalking, see the review by C. L. Scott *et al.* in *Stalking* (ed. D. A. Pinals) (Oxford, 2007), 195-226.

15. The leading authority on the history of stalking is Mullen *et al.*, *Stalkers and their Victims*, 14-7 and 251-2.

16. L. M. Alcott, *A Long Fatal Love Chase* (New York, 1995); there is a review of the book by Stephen King in *The New York Times*, 10 September 1995.

17. *The Morning Chronicle*, 25 December 1838.

18. *The Era*, 21 June 1840.

19. *Examiner*, 1 August 1846; *Freeman's Journal*, 12 and 15 August 1846; *Northern Star*, 6 March 1847. The poem is in *Daily News*, 1 March 1847.

20. *Reynolds's Newspaper*, 31 July 1853; *The Morning Chronicle*, 1 August 1853.

21. *Reynolds's Newspaper*, 13 and 20 July 1856.

22. On Rowdon, see *Reynold's Newspaper*, 27 July 1885; *Morning Post*, 28 July 1885 and 2 July 1886. On Sharpe, see *Morning Post*, 10 and 13 November 1890; *The Era*, 7 May 1892.

23. On Eddie Waitkus, see www.waitkus.org, a good website about him and his career.

12 WHAT WAS WRONG WITH LORD MELBOURNE & THE GOVERNMENT?

1. On *habeas corpus*, see E. M. Freeman, *Habeas Corpus* (New York, 2001); also the articles by H. A. Nutting (*American Historical Review* 65 [1960], 527-43) and J.-C. Paye (*Monthly Review* 57, November 2005).

2. There is a good Wikipedia entry on the impressment of sailors. See also the articles by R. G. Usher Jr (*Mississippi Valley Historical Review* 37 [1951], 673-88), A. Steel (*American Historical Review* 57 [1952], 352-69) and D. N. Keller (*American Heritage Magazine* 46(5), 1995).

3. As stated by L. le Marchant Minty (*Medico-Legal Journal* 54 [1985], 29-39). I have found no evidence to disprove him.

Index

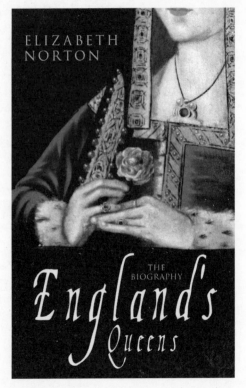